SCHOLASTIC

Reading Skills
Mysteries

**"Whodunits" With Comprehension Questions
That Help Kids Identify the Main Idea, Draw Conclusions,
Determine Cause and Effect, and More**

by DAN GREENBERG

NEW YORK • TORONTO • LONDON • AUCKLAND • SYDNEY
MEXICO CITY • NEW DELHI • HONG KONG • BUENOS AIRES

Teaching
Resources

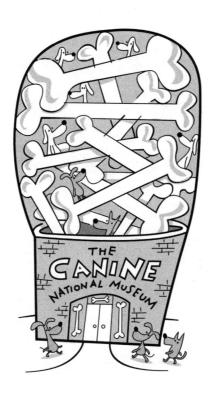

Cover design by Maria Lilja
Illustrations by Jack Desrocher
Interior design by Holly Grundon
Edited by Denise Rinaldo

ISBN 0-439-43764-4
Copyright © 2005 by Dan Greenberg
All rights reserved.
Printed in the U.S.A.

3 4 5 6 7 8 9 10   40   12 11 10 09 08 07 06

Contents

Introduction

Meet Pooch Pearson, a dog private eye who has a knack for sniffing out clever mysteries that help students in grades 3 to 6 improve their reading and writing skills. Pooch Pearson is the star of *FunnyBone Books: Reading Skills Mysteries,* the book you now hold in your hands. Each of the reproducible stories in this book focuses on an important reading skill, such as cause and effect, author's purpose, main idea, and making inferences. Using this book, your students can improve their skills in

- reading comprehension,
- critical thinking,
- problem solving,
- logical analysis,
- creative writing, and
- creative thinking.

Reading Skills Mysteries will help prepare your students for standardized tests, which assess the very same skills these mysteries reinforce. These mysteries are also designed to help you and your students meet the twelve standards for the English Language Arts set forth by the International Reading Association and the National Council of Teachers of English.

But most importantly—because, as all teachers know, a motivated learner is an effective learner—*Reading Skills Mysteries* are fun! Each "case" presents Pooch with a puzzling situation that she somehow manages to solve without ever breaking a sweat. How does Pooch do it?

"Dogs don't sweat," Pooch explains. "They pant."

That being said, please note that a lot of hard work has gone into making this book as fun and useful as possible. Each reproducible story is designed to reinforce a particular reading skill. Ten questions accompany each story, for easy grading and assessment. Stories begin in classic mystery style, opening with a setup that is followed by reading skills questions. The final section of the story presents Pooch's solution to the mystery along with additional reading skills questions. The last question for each story is a writing prompt that links to the story and the skill. For a complete index of all the reading and writing skills in this book, refer to page 64. The answer key starts on page 62.

Please note: Readers who experience a chuckling sensation from these pages should not be alarmed. As Pooch herself has often been known to say: "There is more here than meets the nose."

How to Use This Book

The goal of this book is to use humor to make reading skills less mysterious and more fun for students. Here are some ideas on how to achieve this goal:

1. **BY READING SKILL:** Choose stories according to the key reading skill you wish to cover. See the Skills Index on page 64.

2. **BY WRITING SKILL:** Choose stories according to the key writing skill you wish to cover. See the Skills Index on page 64.

3. **AS AN INTERACTIVE CLASSROOM ACTIVITY:**
   • Read the stories aloud as a class.
   • Have students read in pairs or small groups.
   • Have students work cooperatively to answer the questions and complete the writing exercises.

4. **AS A GAME:** Give students a chance to read the first part of the story. Then encourage them to come up with their own solutions to the mystery before they read Pooch's solution.

5. **AS A WRITING PROMPT:** Invite students to make written responses to the story with questions such as:
   • What did you think of the story's ending?
   • How did Pooch figure out what happened?
   • What were the key clues in the story?
   • What do you think will happen next to these characters?

6. **AS INSPIRATION FOR A CLASS PROJECT:** Invite students to work as a group to create their own Pooch Pearson mysteries, or invent their own unique reading-skill detective.

7. **JUST FOR FUN:** Let students choose how and when to read the stories on their own.

Why I Dislike Cats

An **Author's Purpose** Mystery

★ STARRING ★

Pooch Pearson Private Eye

To solve a mystery, you need to find three things: purpose, purpose, and purpose. It's the same when you're reading. The **author's purpose** is the author's reason for writing something. Sniff out the author's purpose and the rest falls into place. I guarantee it, or my name's not Pooch Pearson!

When people ask why I dislike cats so much I usually say: "Because I'm a dog."

But even if you're not a dog, there's much to dislike about cats. For one thing, cats are too quiet. And though not many humans know it, cats are very poor spellers. But most importantly, cats cause trouble. And I'm not just talking about my notorious archenemy, the evil Tabby Tarkington. No, even everyday cats are troublemakers.

One of my recent cases proves this point *purrrr*-fectly. It all started at Furby's Costume Shop.

My human Rusty and I were picking out our Halloween costumes. I was going as a dachshund—brilliant, don't you think? And Rusty? He was going as an evil dentist. What a pair we were!

This was when a young mouse came up and handed me a note. It was, like all mouse documents, perfectly printed and spelled. The note said: "Please, Ms. Pearson, you've got to help me."

1. **As the story begins, what seems to be the author's (Pooch's) purpose?**
   - ○ **A.** To explain why dogs are smart
   - ○ **B.** To prove that cats are trouble
   - ○ **C.** To explain why cats are likeable
   - ○ **D.** To prove that dogs are smarter than cats

2. **Which of the following statements is most accurate?**
   - ○ **A.** The author wants to give facts to the reader.
   - ○ **B.** The author wants to confuse the reader.
   - ○ **C.** The author wants to persuade the reader of her point of view.
   - ○ **D.** The author wants to persuade and amuse the reader.

3. **What does Pooch say will prove her point about cats?**
   - ○ **A.** A recent report on crimes committed by cats
   - ○ **B.** The events that happened at a recent party
   - ○ **C.** A case that she recently handled
   - ○ **D.** A description of the bad things Tabby Tarkington has done

Now I'm not all that fond of mice, especially the kind that hand you notes, but this fellow at the costume shop seemed genuinely distressed. His name was Larry, and he soon was showing me a letter he'd received from someone who claimed to be his long-lost cousin Bridget. Here it is:

> Deer Cuzzin Larry,
>   You don't no me, but I'm your long-lost cuzzin Bridget. Won't you come to vissit? I'm staying at 254 Feline Street.
>   Yours Trooly,
>   Cuzzin Bridget Mouse

The letter seemed sincere enough, but there was something fishy about it that I couldn't quite put my paw on. Perhaps it was all the spelling mistakes. After all, if there's one thing mice can do, it's spell—unlike cats, most of whom couldn't spell *nine lives* to save their lives.

In any case, it didn't take a genius to recognize that 254 Feline Street was in a bad neighborhood. As far back as I can remember, Feline Street has been a place where cats and kittens prowl around and make trouble.

"That's the problem," explained Larry. "As a mouse, I'm afraid to go there alone. Can you come with me, Ms. Pearson? Can you help me find my long-lost cousin Bridget?" I agreed.

And as I did so, a theory was beginning to form in my head: The letter had been written by a troublemaking cat!

4. **At first, what purpose does the letter's author seem to have?**
   - ○ **A.** To extend an invitation
   - ○ **B.** To persuade
   - ○ **C.** To entertain
   - ○ **D.** To frighten

5. **After considering the clues, what does Pooch begin to suspect is really the author's purpose?**
   - ○ **A.** To help
   - ○ **B.** To teach
   - ○ **C.** To deceive or trick
   - ○ **D.** To advertise

6. **What clue does the letter have to its author's purpose—and true identity?**
   - ○ **A.** Capital letters
   - ○ **B.** Spelling mistakes
   - ○ **C.** A signature
   - ○ **D.** A message in code

We made our way to 254 Feline Street. As a precaution, I went in disguise—wearing the dachshund costume I'd gotten at Furby's. Larry the mouse and I rang the bell while Rusty waited on the sidewalk. A very suspicious-looking—and large!—mouse answered the door.

"We're looking for Bridget Mouse," I said.

"I—uh—I'm Cousin Bridget," replied the large mouse.

The place reeked of cat food. I didn't like it one bit. I explained who we were.

"Cousin Larry!" Bridget cried. "You got my letter! So nice to see you! Come in! Come in. You're so—so—small . . ."

"And you're so big!" Larry exclaimed, ". . . for a mouse."

In fact, for a mouse, Cousin Bridget was enormous. If I hadn't known better, I would have sworn she was the size of a cat! In fact, I suspected that Cousin Bridget was a cat. But how could I prove it?

I had to think of something fast.

"Cousin Bridget," I said. "I wonder if you wouldn't mind spelling the word *impostor* for me."

"Why, no," replied Cousin Bridget. "That would be E-M-P-A-S-T-E . . ."

This was all I needed. "Let's get out of here," I cried. "Run!"

At this point, "Cousin Bridget" made a wild lunge at Larry. Her costume slipped off, revealing a gray tabby-striped fiend. Tabby Tarkington, my archenemy and notorious Feline Street trickster!

I tore off my own dachshund suit, revealing the powerful physique of a fully-grown beagle. The moment he saw me, the dastardly feline turned and, ever the coward, headed for the nearest tree. This allowed Larry to escape back to the sidewalk to where Rusty was waiting with a refreshing chunk of cheese.

As we made our exit, we could still hear the poor loser hissing and snarling from the safety of a high branch.

"You can say that again!" I joked. The three of us had a hearty laugh! **THE END**

7. **This story is funny. That supports the idea that one purpose the author had was to**
   - ○ **A.** entertain.
   - ○ **B.** inform.
   - ○ **C.** solve a problem.
   - ○ **D.** persuade.

8. **This story gives "evidence" that cats are not to be trusted. This supports the idea that the author's purpose was to**
   - ○ **A.** entertain.
   - ○ **B.** inform.
   - ○ **C.** solve a problem.
   - ○ **D.** persuade.

9. **Pooch Pearson says that the purpose of this story was to reveal the "truth" about cats. Why doesn't Pooch seem totally reliable?**
   - ○ **A.** Because Pooch likes cats
   - ○ **B.** Because Pooch doesn't understand cats
   - ○ **C.** Because Pooch was dressed like a mouse
   - ○ **D.** Because Pooch is a dog, and dogs and cats are natural enemies

10. **On a separate sheet of paper, write a paragraph explaining why you prefer either dogs or cats. Make it your purpose to persuade the reader that your point of view is correct.**

Aftermath

We got out of that hideous cat-filled neighborhood as soon as we could. Larry thanked me and we said good-bye. Another case well solved. Which only left Rusty to ask how I knew that "Cousin Bridget" was really a cat.

"That's easy," I replied. "Mice are notoriously good spellers. And cats are bad spellers. When 'Cousin Bridget' failed to spell *impostor*, I knew that was exactly what she was—an impostor!"

"You can say that again!" laughed Rusty.

Pooch's Final Fact

You are what you spell
Or so it appears.
There's no telling
when poor spelling
Can bring you to tears!

The "It's My Party and I'll Cry If I Want To" Case

A **Cause and Effect** Mystery

STARRING

Pooch Pearson
Private Eye

For all you budding private eyes, here's some ace advice: Remember **cause and effect**. The world is a logical place, so things happen for a reason. The reason is the cause. And causes create effects—or results. Keep sniffing, everyone!

My human Rusty and I were at breakfast (kibble for me, eggs Benedict for him) when we heard a knock at the door. "See who that is while I get dressed," I told him. Then I remembered: I'm a dog! I don't need to get dressed. This was when Phil Aardvark burst through the door.

"Sorry to interrupt your breakfast," said Aardvark. "But as you can see, Ms. Pearson, I'm upset. I didn't sleep last night. I was supposed to have this big party. I'd planned everything perfectly. I had the food, I had the party favors, I cleaned, I decorated—but the whole thing was ruined because—"

"No one showed up?" I suggested.

"Why, yes!" he said, amazed. "How ever did you know that, Ms. Pearson?"

"Call it a lucky guess," I joked.

Then I held up *The Morning News*. The headline read: AARDVARK HOSTS BIG PARTY. NO ONE COMES.

"Oh," said Aardvark.

1. EFFECT: Pooch told Rusty to open the door.
   CAUSE:
   ○ **A.** Aardvark yelled.
   ○ **B.** Aardvark rang the bell.
   ○ **C.** Aardvark knocked.
   ○ **D.** Rusty was hot.

2. CAUSE: No one showed up at the party.
   EFFECT:
   ○ **A.** Aardvark was very disappointed.
   ○ **B.** The party was delayed.
   ○ **C.** The party was fun.
   ○ **D.** Aardvark was amused.

3. EFFECT: Pooch knew what had happened with Aardvark's party.
   CAUSE:
   ○ **A.** She read about it.
   ○ **B.** She heard about it.
   ○ **C.** She went to it.
   ○ **D.** A friend told her about it.

"**P**lease sit down, Mr. Aardvark," I said. "Can Rusty get you a refreshment? A bowl of kibble? A dish of ants with a dash of lemon?"

"Sure," replied Aardvark. "I'll have the ants."

Then I asked Aardvark a question that had been forming in my mind. "Mr. Aardvark, did you remember to send invitations to your party guests? I didn't hear you mention anything about them."

At that very moment, I heard a crash. Reaching for a tin of canned ants, Rusty had fallen off our broken ladder. It was the same ladder I'd asked him to fix the day before.

Suddenly, I realized that a single effect can have more than one cause, and that a cause can have more than one effect.

4. EFFECT: Pooch heard a crash. One CAUSE of the crash was that Rusty
   ○ **A.** reached for the tin.
   ○ **B.** was eager.
   ○ **C.** was too careful.
   ○ **D.** purposely knocked down the ladder.

5. A second CAUSE of the crash was that Rusty
   ○ **A.** jumped.
   ○ **B.** argued.
   ○ **C.** laughed.
   ○ **D.** fell.

6. If Aardvark had forgotten to make invitations, one EFFECT would be that the guests wouldn't
   ○ **A.** plan.
   ○ **B.** have appetites.
   ○ **C.** know each other.
   ○ **D.** know about the party.

7. A second EFFECT of forgetting to make the invitations would be that the guests didn't
   ○ **A.** eat.
   ○ **B.** come to the party.
   ○ **C.** have fun.
   ○ **D.** bring presents to the party.

But, in fact, Aardvark had made invitations. "Of course I did!" he cried. "I printed them out myself. Here's a leftover invitation. Take a look for yourself."

The invitation seemed in order: printed clearly, all the important information included—correct address, phone number for R.S.V.P., 34-cent stamp, and so on. I thought. I pondered. I wondered whether I'd stumbled upon a mystery I just couldn't solve. Then, it all clicked.

"I've solved the mystery," I told Aardvark. "Would you like to know why no guests came to your party?"

"Yes, I would!" Aardvark cried.

Solution
Aardvark did everything right—except for one thing.

"**S**tamps don't cost 34 cents anymore! They cost 37 cents!" I exclaimed. And the post office won't deliver mail with insufficient postage.

"So the guests never got the invitations! You've solved the case, Ms. Pearson!" cried Aardvark. "How can I ever thank you?"

"Just send a check made out to Pooch Pearson, Private Detective," said Rusty.

"Of course, I'll do it right away," said Aardvark.

"Oh, and one more thing," I said. "When you mail that check—make sure you use the correct postage!"

We all laughed. And we had a good cause. It was funny!

THE END

Pooch's Final Fact

When friends fail
To get your mail,
Turn on a lamp
And check the stamp!

8. **CAUSE: The invitations didn't have enough postage.**
   EFFECT:
   ○ **A.** The invitations got lost.
   ○ **B.** The invitations weren't addressed.
   ○ **C.** The invitations weren't delivered.
   ○ **D.** Only a few people received their invitations.

9. **CAUSE: Aardvark's friends didn't receive invitations.**
   EFFECT:
   ○ **A.** They got angry with Aardvark.
   ○ **B.** They came early to the party.
   ○ **C.** They didn't come to the party.
   ○ **D.** Aardvark forgot all about the party.

10. Aardvark is planning another party, and this time he's going to personally deliver the invitations to his friends. Imagine that you're Aardvark. On a separate sheet of paper, make an invitation to your party and write a letter to include with the invitation, explaining causes and effects of the earlier invitation mix-up.

The Silver Saucer

A **Sequence of Events** Mystery

STARRING

Pooch
Pearson
Private Eye

Mysteries are like a good game of Go Fish. Shuffle the cards, and nothing makes sense. Find the correct order of things, or **sequence of events**, and it all becomes clear!

It's tough being two things at once. Take myself. Sure, I'm a world-class private eye. But I'm also a dog. Sometimes the two get in the way of each other.

Take, for example, last Thursday. I was at the 34th Annual Gumshoe Awards Banquet with my good pal Chazz Barksdale. We got there just before dinner—an elegant selection of premium "pet" foods.

The Gummies are given each spring to the best private eyes in the city. This year, as usual, I was up against my archrival Tabby Tarkington for the Silver Saucer—the big award given to the year's best detective.

Then, just after dinner, when it was time to give out the award, two strange things happened.

First, there was a power outage. The lights went dark for about five minutes. Someone announced that the blackout had been caused by a faulty air conditioner upstairs in Room 303. I remember looking at my watch when the lights came back on. It was exactly 8:15 P.M. Then, at that very moment, the doorbell in the entry hall rang.

The doorbell!

Now in most situations I'm as cool as the other side of a pillow. But doorbells are different. When dogs hear doorbells, they bark. Period. There's no getting around it.

So I barked.

And kept barking. The guy at the door turned out to be a deliveryman from Snarky's Pizza. What was he doing there? But before I could even begin to figure it out, they suddenly announced from the stage:

"And the winner is . . . POOCHFORD PEARSON!"

Me!

Cool as a cucumber, I strode up to the stage to collect my award. But it was gone! In all the confusion, someone had snatched the Silver Saucer!

At this point, things got even more confusing. The police showed up. Tabby Tarkington offered to help them with the investigation. Quicker than you can say "framed," the police arrested my pal Chazz Barksdale for the theft of the Silver Saucer.

"Pooch, you've got to help me!" Chazz cried as they led him away. "I'm innocent!"

1. **Pooch and Chazz arrived at the Gumshoe Awards banquet**
   - ○ **A.** during dinner.
   - ○ **B.** after dinner.
   - ○ **C.** before dinner.
   - ○ **D.** after the power outage.

2. **The Silver Saucer award was presented**
   - ○ **A.** just before dinner.
   - ○ **B.** just after dinner.
   - ○ **C.** the morning after the banquet.
   - ○ **D.** during dessert.

3. **When did the lights go out?**
   - ○ **A.** At about 7:30
   - ○ **B.** At about 8:00
   - ○ **C.** At about 8:10
   - ○ **D.** At about 9:00

4. **Which event happened immediately before the award was presented?**
   - ○ **A.** Chazz stole the Silver Saucer.
   - ○ **B.** The lights went out.
   - ○ **C.** The doorbell rang, causing Pooch to bark.
   - ○ **D.** The police arrested Chazz.

5. **When are the Gumshoe Awards held?**
   - ○ **A.** In the spring
   - ○ **B.** Every month
   - ○ **C.** In the summer
   - ○ **D.** In the fall

Well, before long, the police found a menu for Snarky's Pizza and a key to Room 303 in Chazz's jacket pocket. This made it look like Chazz caused the blackout and ordered the pizza to distract everyone while he stole the Silver Saucer.

"I didn't do it!" Chazz cried. "Someone must've planted those things on me. I'm innocent!"

I could think of only one way to help Chazz. I called the police. "Be at Gumbo's tomorrow at 7," I told them.

Gumbo is a pal of mine. He owns Gumbo's Milk Pail Restaurant. Every fourth Friday, Gumbo's holds a Bring Your Own Saucer Night. On BYO Saucer Night customers bring in their own saucers, and Gumbo fills them with milk—no matter how large the saucers are!

"The real thief will be at Gumbo's," I told the cops. "If I'm wrong, you can go ahead and charge Chazz Barksdale with the crime."

6. **What evidence against Chazz did the police find first?**
   - ○ **A.** The Silver Saucer
   - ○ **B.** A written confession
   - ○ **C.** Fingerprints
   - ○ **D.** A pizza menu and a key

7. **After the Bring Your Own Saucer Day Pooch describes in this story, when is the next Bring Your Own Saucer Day likely to be?**
   - ○ **A.** Tomorrow
   - ○ **B.** Next Friday
   - ○ **C.** Four Fridays away
   - ○ **D.** Next Monday

We all gathered at Gumbo's the next day. Sure enough, at 7 P.M. sharp, a mysterious stranger wearing a long coat shoved a suspicious-looking saucer onto the counter.

"Fill 'er up," he said.

As Gumbo filled the saucer with thick white liquid, I yelled, "Grab him!" The stranger jumped, spilling the white stuff everywhere, slipping out of his coat and disappearing with catlike quickness out a nearby window.

"If you check, you'll find the saucer he put down is the missing Silver Saucer," I told the cops. "And if you go to 254 Feline Street, you can pick up Tabby Tarkington. He's your thief."

"How can you be so sure?" the cops asked.

Solution
How can Pooch be so sure?

Easy. Before Saucer Night began I instructed Gumbo to be on the lookout for suspicious saucers. He agreed that if one showed up, he'd fill it not with real milk, but with thick white library paste instead. And sure enough, when the police got to Tabby's house, he was covered with the sticky stuff. So that proves Tabby was the mysterious stranger.

"But how did you know that Tabby would bring the Silver Saucer to Gumbo's in the first place?" Chazz asked.

"That's easy," I said. "A cat can't resist a big saucer of milk. It's just like dogs and doorbells. They *have* to do it. And the Silver Saucer is about the biggest saucer you've ever seen. Tabby just couldn't control himself!"

THE END

Pooch's Final Fact

Ask me what I know,
I'll give you my two cents:
Pay attention to the time
of things—
The sequence of events!

8. Choose the correct sequence of events:
   1. **The stranger disappeared from Gumbo's Milk Pail Restaurant.**
   2. **Pooch yelled, "Grab him!"**
   3. **Pooch explained to Chazz what happened.**
   4. **Gumbo filled the saucer with paste.**
   ○ **A.** 1, 2, 3, 4
   ○ **B.** 2, 3, 4, 1
   ○ **C.** 4, 1, 2, 3
   ○ **D.** 4, 2, 1, 3

9. Tabby probably planted the menu and key in Chazz's coat
   ○ **A.** shortly before he stole the saucer.
   ○ **B.** the day before the banquet.
   ○ **C.** several weeks before the banquet.
   ○ **D.** about an hour after he stole the saucer.

10. You have just landed a job as a reporter for **The Daily Dish** newspaper. On a separate sheet of paper, write a story that describes the theft of the Silver Saucer at this year's Gumshoe Awards. Be sure to include the five W's—who, what, when, where, and why.

The Dry Water Caper

A **Draw Conclusions** Mystery

STARRING

Pooch
Pearson
Private Eye

Cracking a tough case is like going for a swim. Sometimes you need to stop tiptoeing around and just take the plunge. In other words, **draw a conclusion**, or put the facts together and make a decision about what's what. Do it!

I was taking a snooze on the rug in my office when in stomped George Osby and Nora Nash. They're both inventors. And they're both hopping mad.

"Hold on!" I told them. "One at a time." But they both started gabbing at about a hundred-and-four miles an hour.

"He's ruining my invention!" cried Nora.

"Am not!" George retorted. "You're ruining *my* invention!"

And so on. Back and forth they went. And just what is this amazing invention they were squabbling over?

"We call it 'H_2O-Dry,'" George explained.

"It's dehydrated water," Nora added.

"Dehydrated water?" I asked. "Is that possible?"

Of course, they both answered. It appears that the two of them were partners—and good friends—just a short while ago. Together, they worked out a process to take all the moisture out of water.

"What does that leave you with?" I asked. George handed me a small bottle. I looked inside.

"There's nothing in here!" I exclaimed.

"Exactly," George replied. "H_2O-Dry is water in its most perfect form. It's light, handy, and completely dry. It takes up almost no space. And you can turn it back to liquid water any time you want."

"How do you do that?" I asked.

"Just add liquid water," Nora replied. "Brilliant, isn't it?"

"Hmm," I said.

I wasn't sure. But when you're in the private-eye business, you learn pretty quickly to listen to clients, even when they seem a little, well, batty.

1. **Draw a conclusion about H₂O-Dry. What are you actually left with when you take all the liquid out of water?**
   - ○ **A.** Nothing
   - ○ **B.** Powder
   - ○ **C.** Gas
   - ○ **D.** Ice

2. **Draw a logical conclusion about how valuable H₂O-Dry is as an invention.**
   - ○ **A.** It's a brilliant invention.
   - ○ **B.** It could be valuable invention.
   - ○ **C.** It's a great idea but ahead of its time.
   - ○ **D.** It's a worthless invention.

3. **Based on the evidence so far, draw a conclusion about the two inventors.**
   - ○ **A.** They seem competent and professional.
   - ○ **B.** At this point, they seem foolish.
   - ○ **C.** They might be dangerous.
   - ○ **D.** They are criminals.

4. **Pooch seems to think the inventors are a little crazy. What evidence in the story allows readers to draw that conclusion?**
   - ○ **A.** Pooch's comment that private eyes must listen to all clients, even "batty" ones
   - ○ **B.** The title of the story
   - ○ **C.** The way Pooch looks at George and Nora
   - ○ **D.** Pooch's tone of voice

5. **Make a prediction. How will the world respond to H₂O-Dry?**
   - ○ **A.** It will be a big success.
   - ○ **B.** H₂O-Dry will be laughed at.
   - ○ **C.** H₂O-Dry will be a modest success.
   - ○ **D.** H₂O-Dry will terrify the public.

Anyway, their big problem—the reason they'd come to see me—wasn't how to make H₂O-Dry. It was how to sell it.

"Suppose you're on a hike and you get thirsty," Nora said. "You take out your H₂O-Dry. It's light, compact, handy, easy-to-carry. But now, where do you get some wet water to make it wet again?"

"Where?" I asked.

This is where they disagreed. George wanted to sell wet water separately with H₂O-Dry. Nora thought that people should get their own wet water.

"You're ruining the whole idea!" George exclaimed.

"No, you are!" Nora retorted.

"Enough!" I cried. "I think I've found a solution that will satisfy both of you."

"You have?" they both asked.

Solution
What is Pooch's solution?

Here's what I proposed. Each container of H₂O-Dry should come as a 2-pack— that includes a special BONUS container of wet water!

This way, you'll always have wet water handy, whenever you need it to put the moisture back in your H_2O-Dry.

"That's brilliant!" George exclaimed.

"Why didn't we think of that?" Nora wondered.

There's only one snag. Carrying around two bottles (one wet, one dry) can be clumsy. But George had a solution to this problem.

"Since H_2O-Dry takes up so little space, you can store it in the bottle cap," he told me.

"Right," added Nora. "So now all you need to do is carry around one bottle. If you want a drink, you just crack open the cap, mix the two together, and PRESTO! You have a delicious, refreshing drink whenever you need it."

"Brilliant!" cried George.

"You're a genius!" exclaimed Nora.

The two of them hugged each other. They were friends again. Partners. Pals.

"Thanks to you," they told me.

"Really," I shrugged. "It was nothing."

And off they went, with big smiles on their faces. Another case well solved. But if you ask me, solving this case was a bit like a bottle of H_2O-Dry—it really WAS nothing!

THE END

Pooch's Final Fact

For cooling you down
And quenching your thirst,
Water has no substitute—
It's the wettest stuff on Earth!

6. **Draw a conclusion about the disagreement between Nora and George. Who is right?**
   - ○ **A.** Nora is right.
   - ○ **B.** George is right.
   - ○ **C.** They're both wrong because the invention doesn't make sense.
   - ○ **D.** They're both wrong because they don't understand how rich the invention could make them.

7. **Pooch says, "It was nothing," when the two inventors congratulate her on her smart solution. Pooch truly thinks her solution is nothing, but the inventors think she's using that expression as a way of**
   - ○ **A.** being modest about her great accomplishment.
   - ○ **B.** asking for money.
   - ○ **C.** making a joke about her abilities.
   - ○ **D.** mocking them.

8. **Why did Pooch offer the solution that she did?**
   - ○ **A.** She wanted to make peace between Nora and George.
   - ○ **B.** She thought it would contribute to the development of a valuable new product.
   - ○ **C.** She wanted to trick the inventors.
   - ○ **D.** She wanted to profit from the invention.

9. **What would most people conclude about Pooch's attitude toward the inventors? Did she take them seriously enough?**
   - ○ **A.** No. She should have done some experiments.
   - ○ **B.** Yes. She solved a ridiculous problem with a ridiculous solution.
   - ○ **C.** No. She should have let them talk more.
   - ○ **D.** Yes. She solved their problem and now the product will be a big success.

10. **On a separate sheet of paper, write a paragraph predicting whether H_2O-Dry will be a success. Explain how H_2O-Dry is different from selling bottled water to people who can easily go to a faucet and get some free water anytime they want.**

The Too-Rich Dentist

A **Making Inferences** Mystery

STARRING

Pooch Pearson
Private Eye

In the private-eye biz, the line between success and failure can be as thin as a beagle's whisker. In order to sniff out the truth, you often need to **make inferences**—educated guesses based on what you see and know. And remember how smart you really are. Trust your instincts!

I was sound asleep under the sofa when a guy walked into my office. He was a real nervous type.

"Ms. Pearson," he said. "My name is Beagleman. Jerry Beagleman. I think my wife is a bank robber."

Needless to say, this got my attention. So did the elegant Luxo watch he was wearing on his wrist. It must be worth several thousand dollars.

"My wife gave me this," he explained. "And these."

He showed me a diamond stickpin. Pearl cuff links. An emerald ring.

"Your wife has good taste, Mr. Beagleman," I said. "You should consider yourself a lucky dog."

"Too lucky," Beagleman replied. "We can't afford these things, Ms. Pearson. My wife is a dentist. I'm a cook. We live a modest life. We're modest folks."

"Hmm," I said. "Slow down. Let me ask you a few questions."

1. **Pooch spots an expensive watch on Beagleman's wrist. There are several logical inferences she could make based on what she sees. Which of the following is not a logical inference?**
   - ○ **A.** Beagleman is rich.
   - ○ **B.** A wealthy person gave Beagleman the watch.
   - ○ **C.** Beagleman can't tell time.
   - ○ **D.** Beagleman likes expensive things.

2. **Beagleman went to see Pooch because of an inference he made—that his wife must be a bank robber. On what evidence did Beagleman base this inference?**
   - ○ **A.** The police have been investigating his wife.
   - ○ **B.** His wife has been researching bank alarm systems.
   - ○ **C.** His wife has lost interest in her career as a dentist.
   - ○ **D.** His wife has been buying valuable gifts that she couldn't afford on her regular salary.

3. Beagleman infers that his wife could be a bank robber. Could this inference be true?
- ○ **A.** Yes. It is definitely true.
- ○ **B.** Yes. It could be true, but it is not the only explanation for the facts.
- ○ **C.** No. Beagleman's wife is a dentist, not a bank robber.
- ○ **D.** No. Beagleman's suspicions are totally crazy.

4. Make an inference about what Pooch is thinking.
- ○ **A.** There must be more to the story.
- ○ **B.** She's about to call the police and have Beagleman arrested.
- ○ **C.** She thinks Beagleman is lying.
- ○ **D.** She thinks Beagleman is crazy.

I posed my first question. "Any idea where she could be getting the money for this stuff—aside from bank robbery?"

Beagleman shook his head. "A few years ago," he said, "we did have quite a bit of money. But we spent it all on my wife's singing career. Things didn't go well, Ms. Pearson. I guess we just ran into some bad luck. Finally, my wife made me a promise: She would quit singing forever and focus on being a dentist again."

"Hmm," I said.

He asked me if I'd look into the case. I told him I would.

I spent the next four days checking out Dr. Mitzi Beagleman. After putting in many long hours, I came to one conclusion: If this woman's a bank robber, then she's a lot smarter than I am. She's clean. Totally clean.

When I told this to Beagleman he seemed relieved. But just that day Dr. Beagleman gave him a new set of fancy golf clubs—and he doesn't even play golf!

I decided that the only thing I could do was to pay Dr. Beagleman a visit at her office. I got there and found the waiting room set up like a nightclub! There were soft lights and tables of customers seated around the dentist's chair at the center of the room. Suddenly, the

receptionist came out and announced:

"And now, Dental Associates presents Dr. MITZI BEAGLEMAN, the Singing Dentist!"

What followed almost knocked me out of my chair. There stood Dr. Beagleman, in a star-spangled dentist's uniform, belting out a fabulous medley of toe-tapping tunes—all while wearing a dental face mask, rubber gloves, and filling two bicuspids in her patient's open mouth. The crowd was going wild, cheering for an encore!

5. Make an inference about why Dr. Beagleman hasn't told her husband about her singing in the office.

- ○ **A.** She thinks he's not interested.
- ○ **B.** She fears he'll be angry because she broke her promise not to sing.
- ○ **C.** She wants to surprise him later.
- ○ **D.** She simply forgot to mention it.

6. Why are so many dogs in the office listening to Dr. Beagleman's performance?

- ○ **A.** Because she's a good dentist.
- ○ **B.** Because she's a good singer.
- ○ **C.** Because she is paying them to listen.
- ○ **D.** Because she's handing out free bones.

7. How will Dr. Beagleman feel about Pooch being there?

- ○ **A.** She will be upset because she doesn't like private eyes.
- ○ **B.** She will be upset because she doesn't want her husband to know about her singing.
- ○ **C.** She will be upset because Pooch ruined her song.
- ○ **D.** She will be happy to have another fan.

When it was over, I told her, "That was fabulous, Dr. Beagleman. But didn't you promise your husband you'd never sing again?"

Her broad smile faded. "Who are you?" she asked suspiciously.

I told her. "Your husband thinks you're robbing banks," I said.

She tried to explain. As the "Singing Dentist" she makes so much money she doesn't need to rob banks! People are willing to pay anything to get their teeth fixed and hear a great song at the same time.

This sounded fine to me. The only problem now was what to tell Mr. Beagleman.

"You can't tell him anything," she said. "I promised I'd never sing again. What am I going to do, Ms. Pearson? I'm ruined. The Singing Dentist will never sing again."

"Not so fast," I replied. "I've just thought of a way to solve your problem."

"You have?" she asked.

Solution
How can Pooch solve both problems at once?

I don't like to lie, but in this case, it seemed like I had no choice. I went back to Beagleman and told him, "Your wife's about to be arrested at her office."

"Arrested?" he cried. "It's all my fault. What can we do, Ms. Pearson? I'll do anything to help."

"Anything?" I replied. "Come with me."

As we arrived at the office Dr. Beagleman was just about to start a root canal—while belting out a rousing rendition of "Swanee River."

Beagleman was flabbergasted. "What's going on?" he asked. "Why is my wife singing? I thought you told me she was going to be arrested."

"Just listen," I said. "I'll explain everything later."

Soon Beagleman was beaming with pride. "She's a terrific singer!" he explained.

"And a great dentist, too," I added.

"I feel guilty!" Beagleman exclaimed.

I explained everything. She has been performing as the Singing Dentist for quite some time now—and it has been a huge success. She's been making oodles of money. Out of guilt for breaking her promise, she'd been buying him things. That explained all the fancy gifts.

It also explained why I had to lie to him. I knew he wouldn't have come to hear her sing, but I had to get him to come here somehow.

"No problem," he said.

"Well, in that case," I said, "can you also forgive your wife for breaking a promise she made to you?"

A big smile spread over his face. "You bet I can!" he replied.

8. At the end of the story, Beagleman said he felt guilty. Why?
- ○ **A.** Because he had so many valuable new things.
- ○ **B.** Because he made his wife promise to quit singing.
- ○ **C.** Because he didn't let his wife dance.
- ○ **D.** Because he committed a crime.

9. Why might Dr. Beagleman feel guilty?
- ○ **A.** Because she lied to her husband.
- ○ **B.** Because she lied to her patients.
- ○ **C.** Because she took advantage of her patients.
- ○ **D.** Because she is not really a dentist.

10. Make an inference about the Beaglemans' future. Are their problems over? On a separate sheet of paper, write a paragraph describing what their life will be like in the future.

Pooch's Final Fact

Mysteries, it seems,
Are part physical, part mental—
Except when the solution
Turns out to be dental!

The Mystery of the Canine Museum Thief

A **Main Idea/Supporting Details** Mystery

STARRING
Pooch
Pearson
Private Eye

Recipe for a successful case: identify the **main idea**, then find **supporting details**. Let them simmer in your brain for a while and then, *presto*! The perfect solution to a tough mystery!

THE CANINE NATIONAL MUSEUM

October 10, a quiet Tuesday. I was having a peaceful snooze on the floor of my office when in walked a rather frantic-looking poodle.

"Pooch Pearson?"

"Do I know you?" I asked.

Her name was Poodle Rabinowitz. "It's my brother Sparky," she said. "He works at The Canine National Museum."

"The Canine?" I asked.

The Canine, as it is known, has the largest collection of chewed dog bones in the country. They've got bones from Antarctica. Bones from Tasmania. They've even got bones chewed by dogs that lived in ancient Egypt.

"So what's the problem?" I asked. "Doesn't he like working there?"

"He loves it," she replied. "At least he did until last Friday. That's when a shipment of rare dog bones went missing from the museum. They think my brother stole them!"

"Did he?" I asked.

"Of course not!" she exclaimed. "Sparky's as honest as the day is long. When we were pups, he never once stole a morsel of food from my bowl! But the police found a security videotape that shows Sparky alone in the museum on the day the bones were taken."

"Hmm," I said. She handed me a copy of the tape. On the cover was a peel-off label that said "Friday." Friday was the day the bones were stolen. I put the tape in my VCR. The date on the screen said October 7. I saw a poodle with a brand-new, spiffy haircut.

"That's Sparky," she said.

"Nice haircut," I remarked. "Where does he get it cut?"

"At Boodleman's Salon du Chien," she replied. "We both go there."

I was impressed. I'd been trying to get an appointment at that place for months.

"We have a standing appointment at Boodleman's," she explained. "On the first Saturday of every month." She showed me a receipt dated last Saturday from Boodleman's for haircuts for both herself and her brother.

"Hmm," I said. "Saturday? This is very interesting."

"Does that mean you'll take the case?" she asked.

"Take the case?" I laughed. "If what you're telling me about Boodleman's is true, I've already solved the case, Ms. Rabinowitz!"

"You have?" she asked.

"Of course," I replied. "Sparky is innocent. And I can prove it!"

1. **What is the main idea in the story so far?**
   - ○ **A.** Sparky has stolen some rare dog bones.
   - ○ **B.** Poodle is Sparky's sister.
   - ○ **C.** Sparky is accused of stealing rare dog bones, and his sister says he is innocent.
   - ○ **D.** Poodle wants Pooch's help settling a fight with her brother Sparky.

2. **Which detail supports what the museum officials think?**
   - ○ **A.** A security tape labeled "Friday"
   - ○ **B.** A security tape labeled "Saturday"
   - ○ **C.** Sparky getting a haircut on Friday
   - ○ **D.** A photo of Sparky with the stolen bones

3. **What detail does Poodle offer to support her claim that Sparky is honest?**
   - ○ **A.** He took a lie detector test.
   - ○ **B.** He has worked at The Canine for years.
   - ○ **C.** All poodles are honest.
   - ○ **D.** He never stole her food.

4. **What detail does Pooch imply will be a key to solving the case?**
   - ○ **A.** Sparky is an attractive dog.
   - ○ **B.** Sparky was a well-behaved puppy.
   - ○ **C.** Bones from Antarctica are on display at The Canine.
   - ○ **D.** Sparky got a haircut at Boodleman's on Saturday.

Solution
How does Pooch know that Sparky is innocent?

"**H**ow can you be so sure my brother is innocent?" Poodle asked.

"Easy," I said. "Take a look at this calendar."

I showed her my calendar. "Today's date is Tuesday, October 10. That means that Friday was October 6, not October 7," I explained.

"What does that mean?" she asked.

"It means the label on the videotape must be wrong," I said. "Look at your brother's haircut."

Sure enough, on the videotape Sparky sported a brand-new spiffy haircut. We knew from the receipt that he got his hair cut on Saturday, the 7th, not Friday, the 6th.

"That means the tape must have been made on Saturday—the day after the robbery—not Friday," Poodle said. "And Sparky always works on Saturdays. It's part of his normal schedule!"

"So Sparky is innocent," I said.

"I can't believe it!" cried Poodle. "Can you explain all this to the police?"

"Consider it done," I replied.

Poodle gave me a big hug. "How ever can I thank you, Ms. Pearson?"

"Can you get me a haircut appointment over at Boodleman's?" I asked. "I find it simply impossible to get a reservation over there."

"Consider it done," she replied.

5. **What is the main idea of this part of the story?**
   - ○ **A.** Sparky is guilty, and Pooch can prove it.
   - ○ **B.** Sparky is innocent, and Pooch can prove it.
   - ○ **C.** Sparky is innocent, but Pooch can't prove it.
   - ○ **D.** Poodle is actually the guilty one.

6. **Which key detail helps break the case?**
   - ○ **A.** The day was not written on the tape.
   - ○ **B.** The day written on the tape is correct.
   - ○ **C.** The day written on the tape is wrong.
   - ○ **D.** The date on the receipt from Boodleman's was wrong.

7. **Which key detail helps Pooch make sure that she is right?**
   - ○ **A.** Poodle has a receipt for a haircut on Saturday, the 7th.
   - ○ **B.** Poodle has a receipt for the rare dog bones.
   - ○ **C.** Poodle has a receipt for a haircut on Friday, the 6th.
   - ○ **D.** Poodle has a photo of the hairstyle Sparky wears.

8. **What does Pooch ask Poodle to do for her in return for solving the mystery?**
   - ○ **A.** Write her a check
   - ○ **B.** Get her a bag of gourmet dog food
   - ○ **C.** Take her on a tour of The Canine
   - ○ **D.** Get her an appointment at Boodleman's

9. **Pooch proves Sparky's innocence, but what important question does Pooch not answer?**
   - ○ **A.** What was Sparky doing on Friday?
   - ○ **B.** How can she get an appointment at Boodleman's?
   - ○ **C.** Who actually stole the bones?
   - ○ **D.** Why was Poodle so interested in clearing her brother's name?

10. **You are Sparky. You have set up a meeting with the head of museum security. The main idea you want to communicate to him is that you're innocent. To do that, you have to provide details. Write a paragraph sketching out what you'll say when you meet with the security chief.**

The Mystery of the Missing Ham

A **Compare and Contrast** Mystery

STARRING

Pooch Pearson Private Eye

Some cases are short and sweet, while others seem to take forever to solve. But when you're adding up the clues, remember to **compare and contrast**. The secret often lies in seeing the similarities and differences between things.

I was sitting in the big chair in my office when a shy-looking hound came in.

"Ms. Pearson?"

"Huh?"

"Sorry to wake you, Ms. Pearson," he said. "My name is Sniffy Jenkins."

"You are?" I asked. "I mean— was I asleep?"

Sniffy Jenkins smiled. "You were snoring, Ms. Pearson, if you don't mind my saying so."

"Hmm," I said. We dogs do have a way of dozing off when there isn't much else going on. "What can I do for you, Mr. Jenkins?" I asked.

Sniffy Jenkins told me about his problem. He was a normal dog. He lived on a normal street, in a normal house, with some normal humans. And now he was being taken to Canine Court, accused of a heinous crime: stealing a 20-pound ham from the refrigerator during the Super Bowl.

"Hmm," I said. "This is serious. Grand Theft Refrig." There was no worse crime that a dog could commit. I looked Sniffy Jenkins in the eye.

"Let me ask you one thing," I said. "Did you do it?"

Sniffy Jenkins smiled sheepishly. "Now don't get me wrong, Ms. Pearson," he said. "I like 20-pound hams as much as the next dog. But no, I didn't do it. Somebody took that ham, but it wasn't me!"

"Where were you when the ham was taken?" I asked.

"I was on the sofa," Sniffy said. "Asleep."

"Hmm," I said. "Was anybody else in the room?"

"Just Steve," he said. Steve, Sniffy's so-called human owner, was a big football fan. At the time the ham was stolen, Steve was in the living room, wearing a shirt with the number 56 on it, yelling and screaming a lot at the TV.

This was all I needed to hear.

1. Compare Sniffy to "normal" dogs. In what way is he similar?

- ○ **A.** He likes hams.
- ○ **B.** He likes football.
- ○ **C.** His owner dislikes football.
- ○ **D.** He loves cats.

2. In the dog world, stealing from a refrigerator is a common major crime. In the human world _____ is a common major crime.

- ○ **A.** stealing bones
- ○ **B.** stealing a car
- ○ **C.** stealing dog food
- ○ **D.** dog-napping

3. Compare the activities of Sniffy and Steve when the ham was stolen.

- ○ **A.** Sniffy was watching the Super Bowl; Steve was asleep.
- ○ **B.** Steve was watching the Super Bowl; Sniffy was asleep.
- ○ **C.** Both Steve and Sniffy were asleep.
- ○ **D.** Steve and Sniffy were on a walk together.

4. Use the context to figure out the meaning of the word *heinous*.

- ○ **A.** Horrible
- ○ **B.** Easy
- ○ **C.** Expensive
- ○ **D.** Rear

"**C**an you help me, Ms. Pearson?" Sniffy asked.

"Help you?" I said. "I can do better than that. I can prove that you didn't take the ham, Mr. Jenkins. When are you due in court?"

"In half an hour," he said.

We got to Canine Court just in time. The prosecutor spent two hours building a strong case that Sniffy took the ham. Things didn't appear promising. When it was my turn to present evidence, the judge asked me whom I was going to call as my first witness.

"No one, Your Honor," I repeated.

"No one?" the judge echoed.

The prosecutor objected. Sniffy was confused. But I told him not to worry. In a few minutes he'd be walking out of the courtroom a free dog.

"But how?" Sniffy asked.

5. On what fact do Sniffy and the prosecutor agree?

- ○ **A.** The ham is gone.
- ○ **B.** Sniffy took the ham.
- ○ **C.** A dog took the ham.
- ○ **D.** The ham wasn't really stolen.

6. On what fact do Sniffy and the prosecutor definitely disagree?

- ○ **A.** A dog ate the ham.
- ○ **B.** There was never a ham in the refrigerator.
- ○ **C.** The ham was overcooked.
- ○ **D.** Sniffy took the ham.

Solution
How can Pooch prove that Sniffy is innocent?

"**Y**our Honor," I said, "at this point I'd like to have a videotape of this year's Super Bowl shown to the court."

The prosecutor objected. "This is highly irregular," the judge said. But she allowed it. A few minutes later they wheeled in a TV and turned on the tape.

"I still don't see what this is going to accomplish," the prosecutor, a well-groomed terrier, said.

"Just watch," I said.

Minutes passed. The game started. A commercial was shown. And to tell the truth, I didn't see much after that.

Neither did anybody else in the court—and that includes the judge, the prosecutor, the defendant, and the jury. Why?

Because we all fell asleep.

We slept through the first quarter. We slept through the second quarter. We slept through the halftime shows, the commercials, the third and fourth quarters. Everything.

It was that dull.

When we finally woke up the judge said to me, "There's no way your client could have committed this crime."

"Why not, Your Honor?" asked the prosecutor.

Because, the judge explained, there was no way that any dog, of any type, could have stayed awake long enough during the Super Bowl to sneak off to the refrigerator and steal a 20-pound ham. It just wasn't possible. The human football fan named Steve must have taken the ham.

"Case dismissed!" the judge cried.

Sniffy Jenkins gave me a gigantic hug.

"How can I ever thank you, Pooch?"

I told him I'd think of something—as long as it didn't involve watching the Super Bowl. That was something a dog just couldn't do. **THE END**

7. **How do dogs and humans compare in the way they watch the Super Bowl?**
   - ○ **A.** Dogs like football more than humans.
   - ○ **B.** Most humans watch the commercials during the Super Bowl.
   - ○ **C.** Dogs love the halftime show of the Super Bowl.
   - ○ **D.** Dogs are bored to sleep by the Super Bowl; many humans like it.

8. **At the beginning of the story, Sniffy was facing punishment for a terrible crime. By the end, he**
   - ○ **A.** had cleared his name.
   - ○ **B.** was serving time for the crime.
   - ○ **C.** was searching for the guilty party.
   - ○ **D.** didn't care anymore.

9. **Everyone in Canine Court was a dog, and they all fell asleep during the tape of the Super Bowl. In a human courtroom, ____ would probably have fallen asleep.**
   - ○ **A.** all of the people
   - ○ **B.** most of the people
   - ○ **C.** none of the people
   - ○ **D.** some of the people

10. **On a separate sheet of paper, write a paragraph comparing your own feelings about the Super Bowl to those of the characters in the story. Which character are you most like? Explain.**

Pooch's Final Fact

A dog's idea of a "Super Bowl"
Occurs almost every night;
It's round, plastic, and filled
with kibble
Delicious in every bite!

The Petting Machine

An **Analyzing Plot** Mystery

STARRING
Pooch
Pearson
Private Eye

Like every good story, every mystery has a **plot**. The key to solving the mystery—and to understanding what you're reading—is getting to the bottom of the plot. So set your sniffer to it! Figure out exactly what happened and why. The rest will unfold in a snap.

I was catching a few Z's under the coffee table in my office when the phone rang.

"Pooch Pearson?" said a voice on the other end.

"Who wants to know?" I asked.

"Professor Phillip K. Fido," the voice replied. "The inventor of the Fido Petting Machine."

Now I've heard stories of petting machines before—contraptions that keep petting a dog without stopping. But as far as I can tell, it's just a pipe dream. No one has ever built a petting machine that really worked. And no one ever will.

But tell that to Professor Phillip K. Fido.

"I tell you, my Fido Petting Machine is 100-percent reliable," Fido said to me when he arrived at my office. He then showed me a photo of the machine, and how cleverly it attached to a dog's neck.

"Sounds great," I said. "Where is it?"

"That's just it," he said. "I was giving a demonstration to five prominent business leaders yesterday morning. Three hours later

the thing disappeared. Gone. Vanished without a trace. Can you help me find it, Ms. Pearson?"

"Hmm," I said. "Would it be possible to call in these five individuals to answer some questions?"

"I should say not!" he cried. "These are

important executives. Do you think they have time to be questioned like common criminals?"

"Of course not," I said. So I sent them all a notice, announcing that I'd be serving FREE FOOD in my office that day at 12 sharp.

Needless to say, this did the trick. By 11:59 my office was filled with the five greedy execs, all stuffing themselves with free kibble like there was no tomorrow.

After they'd had their fill, I called them all together: cheapskate Mutt Jeffords, dashing Pupp Puppston, snobbish Honey Winslow, mumbly-mouth Jack Daniel Spaniel, and super-loaded Dina Dachshund.

"Ladies and gentlemen," I announced. "The reason we've brought you here today is not just to give out free food."

"It's not?" Jeffords cried. He was as cheap as a 2-cent stamp.

"No," I said. "Actually, my name is Pooch Pearson, and on behalf of Professor Fido, I'm here to make you an incredible offer. For a price, one of you can invest in Professor Fido's new invention, the Fido Petting Machine that you saw yesterday morning. What are your bids, ladies and gentlemen?"

Mutt Jeffords spoke up first. "Count me in for a hundred thousand," said the notorious cheapskate. "This sounds terrific."

"A hunnert thousand?" drawled Pupp Puppston, the colorful wildcat oil driller, stunt driver, and the only one in the group who had actually earned his fortune on his own. "That's just chump change, Mutt. I'll put up three hundred thousand smackeroos—and that's all my own hard-earned cash, too."

Multi-trillionaire Honey Winslow was next. Her family had been sponsoring failed petting-machine projects for years. But Honey wasn't feeling well. Rubbing what was obviously a sore neck, she quietly excused herself to go to the powder room.

But this didn't stop old mumble-mouthed

Jack Daniel Spaniel from sweetening the pot to five hundred thousand. And finally, Dina Dachshund checked in at a cool million dollars.

"That's too rich for my blood," said cheapskate Mutt Jeffords.

"Us, too," said Pupp, Jack, and Honey (who had now returned).

This left Dina Dachshund with the winning bid. Professor Fido quickly took me aside.

"Now what?" he whispered.

Once again, I gathered everyone around. "Dina," I said, "Even though you had the winning bid, I'm afraid we can't deliver the Fido Petting Machine to you. Not yet."

"Why not?" Dina asked.

"Because one of you has stolen it," I answered. "And I know who it is."

---

1. **What is Professor Fido's big invention?**
   - ○ **A.** A dog-food maker
   - ○ **B.** A petting machine
   - ○ **C.** A cat-scaring machine
   - ○ **D.** A ball-throwing machine

2. **Why does Professor Fido go to see Pooch?**
   - ○ **A.** His invention has been stolen.
   - ○ **B.** He wants to become a private eye.
   - ○ **C.** He thinks his girlfriend is seeing another dog.
   - ○ **D.** He wants help keeping his invention secret.

3. **What central problem is Pooch hired to solve?**
   - ○ **A.** Whether petting machines work
   - ○ **B.** Whether investors should risk their money on the petting machine
   - ○ **C.** Who stole the petting machine
   - ○ **D.** Whether pet stores should carry the petting machine

4. What is the first step Pooch takes to try to solve the mystery?
- ○ **A.** Pooch invites Fido to her house.
- ○ **B.** Pooch tries the petting machine herself.
- ○ **C.** Pooch offers a reward for the return of the petting machine.
- ○ **D.** Pooch gathers all of the suspects together.

5. Mutt Jeffords uses the figure of speech, "That's too rich for my blood." What does it mean?
- ○ **A.** I don't like sweet things.
- ○ **B.** That is not enough money for me.
- ○ **C.** That is too expensive for me.
- ○ **D.** I am not hungry.

Solution
Who took the Fido Petting Machine?

The room went silent. It was an incredibly tense moment.

"Well, who did it?" asked Mutt Jeffords.

"Yay-ah, Pearson," drawled Pupp Puppston. "If you're so smart, tell us who done it."

"Please," begged Dina Dachshund. "Tell me who took my machine."

I looked at Honey. "It's over, Honey," I said. "Why don't you just give back the petting machine? It'll save us all a lot of trouble."

Honey laughed nervously. "You think *I* took the machine? That's nonsense, Ms. Pearson. What evidence do you have?"

"A pain in the neck, Honey," I said.

"This is too much!" Honey protested. "First, you insult me by calling me a thief. Then, you insult me by calling me a pain in the neck."

I laughed. "I'm not calling you a pain in the neck, Honey," I said. "I'm saying that your obvious painful neck is what clinched the case."

"Huh?" everyone said.

"It's simple," I explained.

During the bidding, I'd noticed that

Honey's neck was sore. This could mean only one thing: that Honey had stolen the machine and had been up half the night massaging her neck with it.

"Ha!" said Honey. "If I've been massaging my neck all night, then why is it still sore?"

"Isn't it obvious?" I replied. "Because the petting machine simply does not work! It made your neck feel worse, not better."

"Now wait a minute here, Pearson!" roared Professor Fido. "That's not true! My machine is 100-percent reliable!"

"I'm afraid not, Professor Fido," I said. "I've done quite a bit of reading on petting machines and frankly, they don't work.

If they did, we'd have replaced human beings with them long ago."

"Why, that's ridiculous!" cried Professor Fido.

"No, Ms. Pearson's right," said Honey. "I'll admit, my family has been searching for a petting machine for years. Yesterday afternoon, I sneaked back to the workshop to try the machine. When Professor Fido unexpectedly came in, I had no choice but to run out the back door with the machine still strapped to my neck."

"You stole my machine!" Dina Dachshund exclaimed.

"It was a mistake, I'm telling you," replied Honey. "I just wanted to borrow it. And it didn't work. You can have it back now, as far as I'm concerned."

This pretty much closed the case. There was only one thing left to explain: Do petting machines really work?

Put it this way: As much as dogs would love someone to invent a working petting machine, think of the consequences. Human beings would be obsolete! What would we need them for anymore?

So if you're like me—I'm sort of fond of humans—you better hope that inventors like Professor Phillip K. Fido aren't successful. Otherwise the honeymoon is over for humans. They'll be on their own again!

THE END

Pooch's Final Fact

Be careful what you wish for—
You may, in fact, get it.
And very soon,
all you may think
Is how much you regret it!

6. **What key detail helped Pooch solve the mystery?**
   - ○ **A.** Honey Watson's neck pain
   - ○ **B.** Dina Dachshund's shoes
   - ○ **C.** Professor Fido's research
   - ○ **D.** Mutt's confession

7. **How was this key detail used to solve the central problem of the plot?**
   - ○ **A.** Scuff marks on Dina's shoes indicated that she had taken the machine.
   - ○ **B.** Professor Fido's nervousness proved that the machine had never been stolen in the first place.
   - ○ **C.** Honey's sore neck indicated that she had taken the machine and had been using it.
   - ○ **D.** Mutt's confession matched the rest of the facts.

8. **What other fact was key in Pooch's solution?**
   - ○ **A.** Petting machines are expensive.
   - ○ **B.** Petting machines don't work.
   - ○ **C.** Petting machines are easy to steal.
   - ○ **D.** Petting machines work only for cats.

9. **Pooch uses the figure of speech, "the honeymoon is over." What does she mean?**
   - ○ **A.** Dogs will no longer receive tough treatment.
   - ○ **B.** Dogs will no longer receive easy treatment.
   - ○ **C.** Dogs will no longer receive any treatment.
   - ○ **D.** Humans' good treatment by dogs is over.

10. **Suppose someone invented a petting machine that did work. On a separate sheet of paper, write an advertisement about the machine that will be aired on WOOF-FM— the leading dog radio station. Use your imagination.**

The Eight-Cent Solution

A **Fact vs. Opinion** Mystery

STARRING

Pooch
Pearson
Private Eye

Just the facts. That's what you want if you're a private eye tracking down clues. So it's important to know the difference between **fact** and **opinion**. Facts can be proven true—the sky is blue, a dog has fur. Opinions express the way a person (or dog) feels about something—cats are the world's most evil creatures. Remember the difference!

I was at my favorite restaurant—Garbaggio's—about to bite into a delicious plate of grits and gristle with picked-over potatoes, when I suddenly heard the sounds of a dispute in the kitchen.

The owner of the restaurant, Nick Garbaggio, was exchanging heated words with Donatello Bowser of Donatello's, the restaurant for humans upstairs.

Here was the problem: Garbaggio's is a dog restaurant. It serves 100-percent leftover food. When Donatello's upstairs throws out its leftovers, Garbaggio's picks them up and serves them to its hungry dog customers—like me!

In the past, this had been no big deal. After all, dogs love leftovers. But now that Garbaggio's was becoming a popular and successful spot, Donatello's wanted in on the deal.

"Why should I give you my leftovers for free?" Donatello asked.

"Because you're throwing them away," Nick said.

"So what?" Donatello replied. "It's still my food."

And so it went, back and forth. Finally, Donatello said, "If only there were someone here that we both trusted."

They looked over toward my table.

"Hey, wait a minute," Nick said. "You know who that is, Donatello? It's Pooch Pearson."

"The famous detective?" Donatello asked.

"The very one," Nick replied. "Let's go ask her to decide this problem."

---

1. Which statement is an opinion?
- ○ **A.** Garbaggio's is a dog restaurant.
- ○ **B.** Grits and gristle is a delicious dish.
- ○ **C.** Garbaggio's serves leftover food.
- ○ **D.** Donatello's is a human restaurant.

2. Which statement is a fact?
- ○ **A.** Both Nick and Donatello trust Pooch.
- ○ **B.** Everyone should trust Pooch.
- ○ **C.** Garbaggio's is a great place for dogs.
- ○ **D.** Leftovers are delicious.

o after the restaurant closed, they came over and explained the whole thing to me.

"I'm just a private eye," I told them. "Not a judge."

"But surely you have some opinion on the matter," said Nick.

"You're right," I said. "I do have an opinion. But you're not going to like it one bit, Nick."

"Well, what is it?" asked Donatello.

"I think Nick should compensate Donatello fairly for the leftovers he gets," I said.

Donatello beamed. Nick was furious.

"Oh, thank you, Ms. Pearson!" Donatello exclaimed. "I knew you'd be fair. How can I ever thank you?"

"Oh, I'm fair all right," I said. "But I'm not so sure, when all is said and done, that you'll still be thanking me."

"Oh, no?" Donatello said. "Whatever do you mean?

"Yeah," said Nick. "Whose side are you on, Pearson?"

---

3. **Which of these statements is NOT an opinion?**
   - ○ **A.** Nick gets his leftover food for free.
   - ○ **B.** Nick is cheating Donatello.
   - ○ **C.** Nick is not cheating Donatello.
   - ○ **D.** Nick should pay Donatello something for the leftovers.

4. **Which of these statements is NOT a fact?**
   - ○ **A.** Pooch is a private eye, not a judge.
   - ○ **B.** Garbaggio's is a successful restaurant.
   - ○ **C.** Nick should pay something for the leftovers.
   - ○ **D.** Donatello thinks Nick should pay for the leftovers.

5. **Pooch says, "I'm just a private eye, not a judge." Is that statement a fact or an opinion?**
   - ○ **A.** Fact
   - ○ **B.** Opinion

Solution
Whose side is Pooch on? How should the case be decided?

"In my eyes," I said, "you should pay for what you get. The payment should suit the purchase. Do we all agree on that?"

"Sounds fair to me," Donatello replied.

"Me, too," said Nick. "Leftovers aren't worth anything, so I shouldn't have to pay for them."

"Not quite," I said. "Leftovers are what's LEFT OVER. So you should pay for them with the money you have left over. Does that sound fair?"

They both nodded.

"Check the cash register, Nick," I said. "How much money did Garbaggio's pull in tonight?"

"We empty out the cash register every night," Nick remarked.

"Why don't you check to see if there's any leftover money in there," I suggested.

Nick opened the cash register. "There is some leftover money," he said. "Eight cents."

"Perfect," I said. "Eight cents is your leftover money. So THAT is exactly how much you should pay Donatello."

"EIGHT CENTS!" Donatello exclaimed. "This is outrageous!"

"True," I said. "But you wanted me to be fair. And what could be more fair than paying for LEFTOVER food with LEFTOVER money?"

At this point, Donatello walked out, fuming with anger. He never did collect his eight cents. Oh, well. If he had, I probably would have taken a cut of it for my fee. After all, when you take a leftover case, what else should you expect but a leftover payment?

Pooch's Final Fact

What's garbage to some folks
To others is treasure.
I guess it depends on
The way that you measure.

---

6. Nick says, "Leftovers aren't worth anything." Is that statement a fact or an opinion?
- ○ **A.** Fact
- ○ **B.** Opinion

7. Which of these statements is a fact?
- ○ **A.** No one should pay for leftovers.
- ○ **B.** The payment should always fit the purchase.
- ○ **C.** Donatello ended up angry.
- ○ **D.** Pooch's decision was fair.

8. Which of these statements is an opinion?
- ○ **A.** Nick empties the cash register every night.
- ○ **B.** The leftover money amounted to eight cents.
- ○ **C.** Pooch's decision was fair.
- ○ **D.** Donatello left the restaurant angry.

9. Which of these statements is NOT a fact?
- ○ **A.** Pooch solved the case.
- ○ **B.** Donatello never collected his eight cents.
- ○ **C.** Pooch determined how much Nick should pay Donatello.
- ○ **D.** Pooch solved the case brilliantly.

10. You are a judge who has been assigned to review Pooch's decision. Was it fair? On a separate sheet of paper, write your opinion. Give reasons to support your conclusion.

The Case of Love Gone Wrong

A **Reading for Details** Mystery

STARRING
Pooch
Pearson
Private Eye

Pooch Pearson is my name, **reading for details** is my game. It's worked for me, a private eye, and it'll work for you, too. Pay attention to the little things, and the big things often take care of themselves.

As a dog private eye, I normally don't take cases that involve humans. But when an old friend of mine named Bobo got me involved in a case with a human named Robert Olson, I felt I had no choice.

Robert "Bob" Olson was the "owner" of Bobo the dog. As if a human could "own" a dog! Ha! Bob was lonely. Through a dating service, Bob met a nice young woman named Millie. The two went on a date. Bob felt that everything went well—great, as a matter of fact. Then, the following day Bob received a note that said:

Shall I compare thee, Bob,
to a summer day?
Pure in heart and pure in hand
You smell just like
A garbage can!
— With Love, A Friend

Well, you human readers can imagine how Bob felt! Apparently, being compared to a garbage can is not such a great thing for a human.

Who would've guessed?

Anyhow, Bob spent the next few days moping around, feeling sorry for himself because he thought Millie didn't like him. This drove his dog, Bobo, crazy. So finally Bobo gave me a call.

"Can you help Bob?" Bobo asked. "Can you find out why Millie wrote such a nasty note to him?"

"Nasty?" I said. I thought it was a lovely note. So did Bobo, actually. But then again, neither of us is human.

"By the way," I asked, "does Millie have a dog?"

"She sure does," said Bobo. "How did you know? Her name is Ruffles and she has a mad crush on me. Or so I thought. But look at this awful note that she sent to me on the very same day."

Shall I compare thee, Bobo,
to a summerday?
Pure in hart and tall you stand
The lovelyest flower
In all the land!
— With Luv, A Frend

"Ugh!" I cried. "A flower! That's disgusting!"

"Tell me about it," said Bobo. "What dog wants to be compared to a sweet-smelling flower? But you can see it's written to me, Bobo."

"Hmm," I said. "It's almost as if they sent the wrong notes on purpose. Do Millie and Ruffles have a computer at their house?"

"Sure," said Bobo. "A very new, fancy one. They write everything on it."

I looked at both notes. Then I looked at Bobo.

"What would you say," I asked, "if I told you that Millie is actually crazy about Bob?"

"I'd say, this better be good," Bobo replied.

1. **Why was Bob unhappy?**
   - ○ **A.** He thought that Millie sent him a nasty note.
   - ○ **B.** He sent Millie a nasty note by accident.
   - ○ **C.** He sent Millie's dog a note by mistake.
   - ○ **D.** He couldn't find a girlfriend.

2. **Why was Bobo upset with the note that he thought was sent to him?**
   - ○ **A.** It compared him to a garbage can.
   - ○ **B.** It insulted his owner.
   - ○ **C.** He didn't like garbage.
   - ○ **D.** It compared him to a flower.

3. **As the narrator, what tone does Pooch take toward the idea of humans owning dogs?**
   - ○ **A.** She likes the idea.
   - ○ **B.** She thinks the idea has a flaw.
   - ○ **C.** She thinks the idea is ridiculous.
   - ○ **D.** She is confused by the idea.

4. **Use the context to figure out a definition for the term _moping around_.**
   - ○ **A.** Acting sad and without energy
   - ○ **B.** Acting bright and energetic
   - ○ **C.** Acting mysteriously
   - ○ **D.** Limping

5. **Make an inference based on things Pooch has said. How will she probably solve the case?**
   - ○ **A.** She will show that Bobo is not telling the truth.
   - ○ **B.** She will show that Bob is lying about the notes.
   - ○ **C.** She will show that the notes were sent to the wrong individuals.
   - ○ **D.** She will prove that a stranger wrote the notes.

Solution
How can Pooch prove that Millie likes Bob?

"It's all based on the computer," I explained.

"Computers don't write notes on their own," Bobo remarked. "Writers write notes."

"True," I said. "But computers do the spell checking on notes. And one thing is very clear about these two notes. One was spell checked. The other wasn't."

Bobo looked at the notes. Sure enough, the "garbage can" note was free of errors. The "flower" note was not.

"Watch what happens when I type the note that you thought was to you, and spell check it on a computer," I said. "Look at the corrections it makes."

Shall I compare thee, Bob,
to a summer day?
Pure in heart and tall you stand
The loveliest flower
In all the land!
— With Love, A Friend

"Wow," Bobo remarked. "It changed 'Bobo' to 'Bob.' That means the flower note was meant for Bob, not for me."

"Exactly," I said.

"But what about the garbage note?" Bobo asked. "The note that Bob thought was for him?"

"That note was from Ruffles to you," I replied. "It was run through the spell checker so it has no mistakes. Except that the spell checker didn't recognize the name 'Bobo,' so it changed it to 'Bob,' which it did recognize."

"By gosh, you're right again!" Bobo cried. "So the note I got, about the icky flower, was intended for Bob, while the note Bob got, about smelling like a garbage can, was really for me."

"You got it," I said.

"You're the best, Pooch," Bobo said to me, giving me a big hug.

"Hey," I shrugged. "What are friends for?"

THE END

Pooch's Final Fact

It's better to
Have loved and lost,
Unless you are the one
Who got double-crossed!

---

6. **What key detail helped Pooch solve the case?**
   ○ **A.** The spell checker changed *Bob* to *Bobo*.
   ○ **B.** The spell checker changed *Bobo* to *Bob*.
   ○ **C.** The spell checker changed *garbage* to *flower*.
   ○ **D.** The spell checker changed *Luv* to *Love*.

7. **Compare the ways that dogs and people in this story feel about smelling like garbage.**
   ○ **A.** Dogs think smelling like garbage is great; people don't.
   ○ **B.** Dogs and people both think garbage is great.
   ○ **C.** Dogs and people both think smelling like garbage is disgusting.
   ○ **D.** Dogs love garbage; people are indifferent to it.

8. **How did Pooch know that the "garbage" note had probably gone through the spell checker?**
   ○ **A.** It changed the name *Bobo* to *Bob*.
   ○ **B.** It had no spelling errors.
   ○ **C.** It was written by a human being.
   ○ **D.** It said so at the bottom.

9. **Make a prediction. How will Bob feel when he hears Pooch's solution to the mystery?**
   ○ **A.** Angry
   ○ **B.** Confused and worried
   ○ **C.** Uninterested
   ○ **D.** Happy and relieved

10. **On a separate sheet of paper, write a letter that Bob might write to Millie explaining the whole situation. Make sure the letter summarizes what happened.**

The Hat Ed Caper

A **Cause and Effect** Mystery

STARRING
Pooch
Pearson
Private Eye

When you're trying to sniff to the bottom of things, remember **cause and effect**. The effect, by the way, is a thing that happens. The cause is the reason why. It's something a good private eye just can't forget.

I never dreamed I'd be in the movies. So when two well-known movie people came rushing in to my office, waking me up from a sound sleep, I took notice.

"Ms. Pearson," they said. "You've got to help us."

Gus Ross and Flo Pomeranian were a successful Hollywood screenwriting team. I'd enjoyed several of the movies they'd worked on, especially the ones with Ed Doberman, the brilliant director.

"I love those Ed Doberman films," I said.

"So do we," replied Flo. "I think they're our best work by far. We love working with Ed!" And they were about to start a new project with Ed Doberman just this last week.

"So what happened?" I asked.

"Well, as you may know," Gus said, "Ed Doberman is just coming out with a new movie that he wrote himself."

"It's called *The Hat Ed Show*," Flo continued. "It's about a dog named Ed who wears many different hats. It's the first movie that Ed's ever written, directed, and also starred in himself."

"Sounds terrific," I said.

"It is terrific!" Gus exclaimed. "And that's what we told Ed when he sent us a DVD of *The Hat Ed Show* to preview—that we really liked the movie."

"So what's the problem?" I asked. The two looked at each other.

"After we sent him the card congratulating him for *Hat Ed*, something went wrong," Flo replied. "He refuses to see us. He won't even return our calls."

"Hmm," I said. "Can I see the message you sent?"

"Sure," Gus said. He wrote out this message:

Hat Ed Show BIG!—G. Ross, Flo P.

"You see," Flo said. "We told him we thought the show was really BIG. In Hollywood, Ms. Pearson, that's about the highest compliment you can give—saying something is BIG."

"Hmm," I said. "Are these the exact words you wrote?"

"Well, actually," Flo replied, "I gave the message to our secretary, Walter, to send. He's very reliable—other than sometimes messing up punctuation and spacing. And I wrote the words out very clearly, in capital letters—for Walter to send."

"Hmm," I said. "Have you tried to contact Mr. Doberman since you sent him the message?"

"Yes!" cried Flo. "But again, he won't speak to us. Can you at least get him to talk to us on the phone, Ms. Pearson?"

"I can do better than that," I replied. "I think I can clear up this whole problem."

Gus shook his head. "I don't know, Ms. Pearson," he said. "In Hollywood, problems get solved neatly and there's always a happy ending. But here in real life, solutions are often a lot more messy."

"We'll see," I said.

1. **EFFECT: Flo and Gus came to see Pooch.**
   CAUSE:
   ○ **A.** They needed money.
   ○ **B.** They needed help contacting Ed Doberman.
   ○ **C.** They needed to find Ed Doberman.
   ○ **D.** They wanted to say hello.

2. **CAUSE: Flo and Gus really liked *The Hat Ed Show*.**
   EFFECT:
   ○ **A.** They called Ed on the phone.
   ○ **B.** They wrote Ed a note.
   ○ **C.** They went to Ed's office.
   ○ **D.** They decided to work with Ed.

3. **EFFECT: Ed won't speak to Flo and Gus.**
   CAUSE:
   ○ **A.** The cause is unknown at this point in the story.
   ○ **B.** Ed never liked Flo and Gus.
   ○ **C.** The movie was a failure.
   ○ **D.** Ed couldn't understand the note.

4. **EFFECT: Flo and Gus are upset.**
   CAUSE:
   ○ **A.** They don't like Ed's movie.
   ○ **B.** They don't like each other.
   ○ **C.** They can't get in touch with Ed.
   ○ **D.** They can't find a new job.

Solution

How can Pooch solve the problem?

"It's simple," I explained. "Ed Doberman just misunderstood your message."

"Huh?" Flo said.

"Here's what you thought you wrote," I said. I used a bunch of alphabet blocks that were sitting in a box in the corner to write out the message. It said that the HAT ED SHOW was BIG and it was signed "G. Ross" and "Flo P."

"But here's what Ed Doberman got," I said.

If the spacing got just slightly changed, here's what got spelled out.

"Oh, my gosh!" yelped Flo. "Ed thought we told him that his show was a BIG GROSS FLOP!"

"No wonder he was angry!" Gus exclaimed. "We can clear up this whole thing if we can get somebody to go over there and explain it to him."

"I suppose I could do that," I said.

"Would you?" cried Flo.

"Why, sure," I remarked. "I've always wanted to be in pictures. This could be my big chance."

THE END

Pooch's Final Fact

If you make a flop in Hollywood
No one remembers your name,
Unless you happen to be a star
Or someone who can take the blame!

---

5. **CAUSE: Walter, the secretary, has a hard time with spacing and punctuation.**
    EFFECT:
    - ○ **A.** He got extra help in language arts.
    - ○ **B.** He bought a book about punctuation.
    - ○ **C.** He wrote the note to Ed very carefully.
    - ○ **D.** He made big mistakes in the note to Ed.

6. **EFFECT: The message spelled out a "big gross flop."**
    CAUSE:
    - ○ **A.** There were spelling mistakes.
    - ○ **B.** Someone changed the message.
    - ○ **C.** The letters and spaces got rearranged.
    - ○ **D.** The assistant wanted to play a trick.

7. **CAUSE: Ed felt insulted by Flo and Gus.**
    EFFECT:
    - ○ **A.** Ed sent Flo and Gus a nasty note.
    - ○ **B.** Ed became friends with Flo and Gus.
    - ○ **C.** Ed tried to replace Flo and Gus.
    - ○ **D.** Ed refused to talk to Flo and Gus.

8. **CAUSE: Pooch figured out what had happened.**
    EFFECT:
    - ○ **A.** Flo and Gus were worried.
    - ○ **B.** Flo and Gus were happy.
    - ○ **C.** Flo and Gus wrote a new note.
    - ○ **D.** Flo and Gus got into an argument.

9. **EFFECT: Pooch went to explain the situation to Ed.**
    CAUSE:
    - ○ **A.** Ed didn't like Pooch.
    - ○ **B.** Ed said he wanted to meet Pooch.
    - ○ **C.** Ed never liked Pooch.
    - ○ **D.** Ed still wouldn't speak to Flo and Gus.

10. **You're a Hollywood scriptwriter. On a separate sheet of paper, write a movie scene showing what happens when Pooch goes to explain the misunderstood note to Ed. Write your scene in dialogue form.**

The Mystery of Old 81

A **Make Inferences** Mystery

STARRING
Pooch
Pearson
Private Eye

Being a private eye involves lots of guesswork. But that doesn't mean taking a shot in the dark! A good detective, like a good reader, learns to **make inferences**—educated guesses based on the information you have.

I was awakened from a mid-morning slumber by a pounding at my office door.

"Pooch Pearson!" cried a frantic voice.

"Calm down," I said. "What's the problem?"

Only then did I realized that standing in front of me was none other than Lefty Lopez, good old Number 81 of the Bay City Lugs dog football team.

"Lefty Lopez, you big Lug!" I cried. "Long time no see. What brings you here? Aren't you getting ready for the big game against the Yowlers on Sunday?"

"I wish I could," said Lefty. "But I can't play. I'm banned from the game."

"Banned?" I cried. "How could that be?"

He explained. In last week's game, too many players were performing wild victory dances after touchdowns. Finally, the referees issued a warning: The next player to do a victory dance will be banned from the following week's game!

"And that was you?" I asked. "I can't believe it."

"Neither can I," replied Lefty. "But take a look."

Lefty handed me a photograph from the newspaper. There was Old Number 81 doing a victory dance at the end of the game. You couldn't see the player's face, but the number 81 in green and gold was clearly visible—so it had to be Lefty.

Or did it? I looked closely at the picture. The player in the picture was spiking the bone-shaped football into the ground with his left paw.

"The picture's a fake!" Lefty exclaimed. "I'm sure of it!"

"I'm afraid not," I replied.

"Are you calling me a liar?" Lefty huffed.

"Not at all," I remarked. "I said the picture's not a fake. But I didn't say it was you!"

"Huh?" Lefty was confused. He was starting to bark in spite of himself.

"Why don't you just calm down," I said, "and save your energy for the big game?"

"The big game?" Lefty repeated. "You mean I'm going to play in the big game after all?"

"Of course you're going to play," I said, "or my name's not Pooch Pearson."

Solution
How can Lefty play in the big game?

"Look closely at the photo," I said. "What do you see?"

"A guy wearing No. 81 spiking the bone," Lefty responded. "The helmet covers his face so you can't tell who he is."

"Correct," I said. "Which paw is he spiking with?"

1. **Make an inference about the relationship between Pooch and Lefty.**
   - A. They're old pals.
   - B. They have never met before.
   - C. Pooch knows Lefty only from reading about him in the newspaper.
   - D. Pooch and Lefty are cousins.

2. **What helped you make your inference for question 1?**
   - A. Pooch does not use Lefty's first name.
   - B. Pooch says, "Long time no see."
   - C. Pooch calls Lefty a lug.
   - D. Pooch calls Lefty, "Cuz."

3. **Make an inference about performing a victory dance in a dog football game.**
   - A. Players are supposed to perform victory dances.
   - B. Performing a victory dance is against the rules.
   - C. No one ever performs a victory dance.
   - D. Players are judged on the quality of their victory dances.

4. **When the referees saw the newspaper photo of Number 81 spiking the ball, what did they infer?**
   - A. The player was Lefty.
   - B. The player was not Lefty.
   - C. Someone was trying to get Lefty banned from the big game.
   - D. The newspaper printed an old photo.

"His left," Lefty replied. "And I'm left-pawed."

"But hold on," I said. "If you look closely at the photo, you'll see it's reversed—it's a mirror image. The newspaper printed it backwards. So how can we see it correctly?"

"Uh, I don't know," Lefty said. "Hold it up to a mirror?"

"Bingo!" I replied.

In the mirror, two things in the picture changed. First, the player was clearly shown to be right-pawed, not left-pawed. And more importantly, the number on his shirt was reversed.

"It says 18, not 81!" Lefty cried. "It's not me!"

"You're right," I said.

"Hey, wait," Lefty said. "I remember this now. That's Biff Shepherd—he wears number 18. He ran out and spiked the ball at the end of the game."

"Bingo," I said. "So you're in the clear."

"Wow," Lefty said. "How can I ever thank you?"

"Just go out and win one for the good guys," I replied.

"That's easy," Lefty said. "We ARE the good guys."

I sure couldn't argue about that.

Pooch's Final Fact

Dog football is a game that
Dogs play in the spring and fall.
Why's it so much better than
human football?
You get to eat the ball!

5. **Make an inference about spiking the football.**
   - ○ **A.** Dogs use their mouths to spike.
   - ○ **B.** A left-pawed player uses his left paw to spike.
   - ○ **C.** A right-pawed player uses his left paw to spike.
   - ○ **D.** A player uses one of his front paws to spike.

6. **Make an inference about Pooch's favorite team.**
   - ○ **A.** She likes the Yowlers.
   - ○ **B.** She likes the Yankees.
   - ○ **C.** She has no favorite team.
   - ○ **D.** She likes the Lugs.

7. **Make a prediction about Lefty.**
   - ○ **A.** He will be able to play in next week's game against the Yowlers.
   - ○ **B.** He will change his number to 18.
   - ○ **C.** He will spike the football in next week's game and be banned.
   - ○ **D.** He will try to change the rules about victory dances.

8. **Make an inference about Biff Shepherd.**
   - ○ **A.** He will be the star of next week's game.
   - ○ **B.** He will change his number.
   - ○ **C.** He will change his name.
   - ○ **D.** He will be banned from next week's game.

9. **Make an inference. How will Biff Shepherd feel when he learns about the photo?**
   - ○ **A.** Happy
   - ○ **B.** Cheated
   - ○ **C.** Upset
   - ○ **D.** Amused

10. **You're a sports reporter for *The Daily Bone*. On a separate sheet of paper, write an article reporting on the big Lugs/Yowlers dog football game (the one from which Lefty wasn't banned). Use your imagination to make inferences about how dog football is played.**

The Foggy Mile

A **Reading for Details** Mystery

STARRING Pooch Pearson Private Eye

Details. They're just useless little facts that aren't worth worrying about, right? Wrong! Totally wrong! Especially if you're a private eye—or a top-notch reader. It's those picky little details that come together to form a great story—or the solution to a mystery.

I was trying to catch up on my sleep when into my office strolled a very speedy-looking greyhound.

"Pooch Pearson?" she asked. "I'm Foxie Martinez."

"Of course," I replied. "You're Foxie the Fox. The racer. What can I do for you?"

"I want you to help me prove that I was the winner of last week's Minnesota Mile," Foxie said.

"Hmm," I said. The Minnesota Mile was the biggest dog race of the year. I'd read about it in the papers. Foxie Martinez had been way ahead. Then, at the last moment, Slick Betty Burford came out of nowhere to win the race. The headlines read: SLICK BETTY B. OUTFOXES THE FOX!

What happened was that just before the start of the final lap, a big cloud of fog moved in on the racetrack. No one could see anything. No one knew what to do.

"So we just kept on racing," Foxie explained. "I was ahead when the fog came in. But somehow Slick Betty B. ended up winning."

"How'd she do it?" I asked.

"I don't know," Foxie replied. "It was so foggy, I couldn't see anything. But there's one thing I do know: She never passed me. In fact, no one passed me once the last lap began. Even in that thick fog I would've seen them."

"Hmm," I said for the second time. "Where was Betty on the racetrack when you last saw her?"

Foxie drew a diagram of the track on a sheet of paper.

"She was right behind me as we rounded the turn just before the beginning of the final lap," Foxie explained. "I remember because I was worried about her making a move."

"And then?"

"The fog came in and she just disappeared," Foxie said. "I didn't see her again until the last turn of the final lap, when I got near the finish line. And suddenly there she was, a few yards ahead of me."

"Hmm," I said, for the third time. "And what would you like me to do?"

"Well," Foxie said. "I guess you can't help me win a race that's already over and done with. But maybe you can help me get a rematch with Slick Betty."

"I can do better than that," I said.

"Huh?" Foxie said.

"You beat Slick Betty in last week's Minnesota Mile," I explained. "And I can prove it!"

---

1. **Why does Foxie go to see Pooch?**
   - ○ **A.** She wants Pooch to find Slick Betty.
   - ○ **B.** She wants Pooch to prove the newspapers have a grudge against her.
   - ○ **C.** She wants Pooch to prove that Slick Betty didn't really win the race.
   - ○ **D.** She wants Pooch to prove that dog racing is cruel.

2. **What is Foxie unable to figure out?**
   - ○ **A.** How Slick Betty got ahead of her
   - ○ **B.** Why the newspapers put Slick Betty in the headline
   - ○ **C.** Why she ran so slowly
   - ○ **D.** Why she is so upset

3. **What was unusual about the race?**
   - ○ **A.** Slick Betty was one of the racers.
   - ○ **B.** A big cloud of fog rolled in after the race began.
   - ○ **C.** A big cloud of fog came in after the race was over.
   - ○ **D.** Horses and dogs competed.

4. **What is one thing that Foxie is sure of?**
   - ○ **A.** She won the race.
   - ○ **B.** She lost the race.
   - ○ **C.** No one passed her in the race.
   - ○ **D.** Pooch will solve the case.

5. **How does Foxie want to correct the mistake that was made in declaring a winner?**
   - ○ **A.** She wants a rematch against Betty.
   - ○ **B.** She wants a prize for winning the race.
   - ○ **C.** She wants Betty kicked out of racing for good.
   - ○ **D.** She wants a lifetime supply of bones.

Solution
How can Pooch prove that Foxie won the race?

"It's simple," I said. "Betty won by losing. She just quit running."

"Won by losing? Quit running? Huh?" Foxie stammered.

I showed her on the diagram where the racers started going into the last lap. Foxie was ahead. Betty was in second.

Then the fog came in. Everyone kept running. Everyone, that is, except for Slick Betty.

When the fog lifted, it suddenly looked like Betty was ahead.

But actually, she hadn't moved an inch!

"Of course!" cried Foxie. "Slick Betty won the race by standing still. She didn't run as many laps as the rest of us. That's how she got ahead."

"So you were the real winner," I said.

"I sure was," Foxie said. "And now I can prove it. How can I ever thank you, Ms. Pearson?"

"Ten thousand dollars would be okay," I replied.

"Ten thousand dollars!" she cried.

I was only joking. But wouldn't it be great if I actually could earn that much solving a case? In your dreams, Pooch Pearson. In your dreams!

THE END

Pooch's Final Fact

When running in a race
Remember to bear this in mind:
Keep your eye on what's ahead,
And also on what's behind!

6. **What did Foxie do when the fog rolled in?**
   - ○ **A.** She stopped.
   - ○ **B.** She kept running.
   - ○ **C.** She caught up with Betty.
   - ○ **D.** She started barking.

7. **What did Betty do when the fog rolled in?**
   - ○ **A.** She stopped running.
   - ○ **B.** She ran faster.
   - ○ **C.** She caught up with Foxie.
   - ○ **D.** She started barking.

8. **Why did it seem like Betty won the race?**
   - ○ **A.** Because she ran faster than everyone else
   - ○ **B.** Because she ran more laps than everyone else
   - ○ **C.** Because she ran fewer laps than everyone else
   - ○ **D.** Because she moved the finish line

9. **What helped Pooch figure out what had happened?**
   - ○ **A.** Calling the police
   - ○ **B.** Using a computer
   - ○ **C.** Sleeping on the problem
   - ○ **D.** Drawing a diagram

10. **Draw a conclusion. Did Slick Betty cheat to "win" the race? Or did she end up being declared the winner by accident? On a separate sheet of paper, write a story for the sports section of *The Canine Courier* that explains what happened.**

The Mailman's Revenge

A **Narrator's Voice** Mystery

STARRING
Pooch
Pearson
Private Eye

The narrator is the person who's telling the story. Understand the **narrator's voice**—that one who's telling the story and how it's told—and a lot of things start to make sense. It's true in mysteries, and it's true in reading, too!

There's no worse crime for a dog than to bite a mail carrier. It's the one thing that isn't allowed. I should know. Years ago, I was involved in a mailman case with a dog named Ralph. I got Ralph off, and the mailman, a piggish man named Jason Piggot, swore he'd get revenge.

Little did I know that the revenge would be on me, not Ralph!

It all started the other day. I must have dozed off as I was reading the Sunday paper when there was a knock at the door.

"Special delivery!" a voice called out.

"Hmm," I thought, what an odd time for a package. I wondered what it could be.

Before long, I realized that the package was stuck in the mail slot of the door. Then I looked at the label. It said: TO OPEN, BITE DOWN HARD.

So I bit.

"Yow!" someone cried.

A moment later, the door opened, and a voice yelled, "You're under arrest!"

"Arrest?" I asked. "For what?"

"For biting a federal mail carrier in the line of duty," the voice replied.

Then the "package" in the mail slot pulled out, and proved to be not a package but the right ARM of a mailman. Then I saw that it wasn't just any mailman.

"You're Jason Piggot!" I cried.

"You bit me!" said Piggot, walking around to my side of the door. "You bit a mail carrier in the line of duty. You'll fry for this, Pearson!"

"This is outrageous!" I cried.

"Tell it to the police," Piggot sneered.

A moment later the police arrived. They brought me in before Judge Betty LaFay. I'd always known LaFay to be fair and even-handed.

"What's the charge?" she asked.

"It's as clear as glass, Your Honor," Piggot answered. "The defendant, Ms. Pearson, bit a mail carrier in the line of duty."

"That's ridiculous!" I exclaimed.

But it turned out that when you bite a mailman in the line of duty it counts—even if he was sticking his arm through the door pretending it was a package.

"I'm sorry," Judge LaFay said to me. "Do you have anything to say for yourself, Ms. Pearson, before I pass judgment?"

"Yes, I do, Your Honor," I answered. "I want you to dismiss all charges against me."

"That's impossible!" cried Piggot. "We've got you dead to rights here, Pearson. You're going to jail!"

"Want to bet?" I retorted.

---

1. **Who is the story's narrator?**
   - ◯ **A.** Pooch Pearson
   - ◯ **B.** Jason Piggot
   - ◯ **C.** Judge LaFay
   - ◯ **D.** There is an omniscient narrator.

2. **What voice does the narrator use?**
   - ◯ **A.** The third person
   - ◯ **B.** The second person
   - ◯ **C.** The first person
   - ◯ **D.** The last person

3. **What is the best clue to the fact that Pooch (the narrator) is a first-person narrator?**
   - ◯ **A.** The narrator calls herself "I" or "me."
   - ◯ **B.** The story is a mystery.
   - ◯ **C.** The narrator never uses "I" or "me."
   - ◯ **D.** The story takes place near the present day.

4. **Pooch's stories are actually _____, which are almost always written in the first person.**
   - ◯ **A.** mysteries
   - ◯ **B.** true stories
   - ◯ **C.** funny stories
   - ◯ **D.** memoirs

5. **What is the narrator's attitude toward Jason Piggot?**
   - ◯ **A.** She respects him, but she disagrees with some of the things he does.
   - ◯ **B.** She is terrified of him.
   - ◯ **C.** She has no attitude toward Piggot.
   - ◯ **D.** She dislikes him.

Solution
How can Pooch prove that she is innocent?

"**M**r. Piggot," I said. "Would you mind reading the mail carrier's credo?"

"Sure," laughed Piggot. "'Neither snow, nor rain, nor dark of night shall keep the mail carrier from his or her daily round of duty.'"

"And how would you define the word *daily*, Mr. Piggot?'"

"Every day of the week," Piggot said. "Monday through Saturday. We deliver the mail."

I held up the newspaper I'd been reading at home when Piggot burst in.

"Can you read the line at the very top of the page, Mr. Piggot?" I asked.

"Why, sure," Piggot replied. "It says: Sunday, March 11."

"Since when does the postal service deliver mail on Sundays?" I asked.

"Uh-oh," said Piggot.

"Your Honor," I said, "I move to dismiss this case on the grounds that the mailman was not bitten during his 'round of duty'—since he has no duty on a Sunday. He obviously showed up on my doorstep today with revenge on his mind. His plan all along was to frame me for a crime I would never purposely commit!"

Judge LaFay smiled. "I tend to agree," she said. "Nice job, Ms. Pearson." And then she looked at Piggot. "You would do well to get out of my sight, sir," she said. "And don't come back soon."

THE END

Pooch's Final Fact

Nothing can stop the mail
From being delivered to you,
Except for a barking dog
Who's looking for something to chew.

6. **What is the narrator's attitude toward the judge?**
   - ○ **A.** Fear
   - ○ **B.** Contempt
   - ○ **C.** Disrespect
   - ○ **D.** Respect

7. **How is the narrator's attitude toward the judge supported by what happens in the story?**
   - ○ **A.** The judge deals harshly with Pooch.
   - ○ **B.** The judge deals fairly with Pooch.
   - ○ **C.** The judge tricks Piggot into confessing that he is guilty.
   - ○ **D.** The judge makes up her mind without hearing all the evidence.

8. **What key detail helps Pooch solve the case?**
   - ○ **A.** The arm belongs to Jason Piggot.
   - ○ **B.** The mail is delivered every day.
   - ○ **C.** The mail is not delivered on Sunday.
   - ○ **D.** Jason Piggot confesses.

9. **Which character traits best describe Jason Piggot?**
   - ○ **A.** Dim-witted and slow
   - ○ **B.** Treacherous and mean
   - ○ **C.** Intelligent and misunderstood
   - ○ **D.** Strange and brilliant

10. **How might this story have been different if it had been told by a different narrator? Choose another narrator for the story—Jason Piggot or Judge LaFay. On a separate sheet of paper, briefly retell the story in the first person from that character's point of view.**

The Old Smokey Caper

An **Understanding Character** Mystery

STARRING

Pooch
Pearson
Private Eye

When it comes to cracking a really tough case, character is what counts. If you understand **character**—who your suspects are, what makes them growl, why they do what they do—you're just a whisker away from solving the mystery.

I t seems like every time I settle down for a nice snooze, I get interrupted by some frantic client who desperately needs my help. Today was no different.

"Pooch Pearson?" called the fellow at the door.

"Can I help you?" I asked.

His name was Victor Schnauzer. He was a scientist. He had a snobby voice and was wearing extremely thick eyeglasses. He had been accused of stealing a secret new dog-food formula.

"Did you do it, Dr. Schnauzer?" I asked.

He scowled at me. "Do I look like a thief?" he asked.

I shrugged. Who knows anything anymore? Cheaters look honest. Honest folks often look like scoundrels. In any event, the case seemed simple enough. Victor and rival scientist Katrina van Katson both claimed to have discovered the same secret formula.

"Is that possible?" I asked.

"You must understand," Victor said. "Katrina is an excellent scientist. But she is also a cat. I suspect that she stole the formula from me somehow."

"How did you discover the formula?" I asked.

In his snooty way, Victor explained how they'd both independently been researching the same ingredients. The key step—the step that Victor alone had discovered—was to heat the mixture for exactly one hour at exactly 211 degrees—one degree below boiling.

"Hmm," I said. "Do you both work for the same company?"

"Heavens, no," Victor replied. "I work here in the city at Dogfield Laboratories." I knew the place well. It was down near the docks, by the ocean. "Katrina works at Old Smokey Mountain Labs," he added.

"Isn't that the place on top of Old Smokey?" I asked.

"The very one," Victor answered. "They claim they get better scientific results up there because the mountain air is purer at 10,000 feet."

"Hmm," I said. "Do you think they get better results?"

"I don't know," Victor said. "All I know is that I discovered this formula all on my own. You must believe me, Ms. Pearson!"

This sounded like an order—and I'm not one who likes being ordered around. "Calm down," I said.

"Calm down?" Victor repeated. "I'm not going to calm down until you get to work on this case, Ms. Pearson!"

"If you want to know the truth," I chuckled, "I've already SOLVED the case. I can PROVE that you were the one who invented the formula—and that Katrina van Katson is lying."

"Are you serious?" asked Victor.

"Does a dog like a bone?" I replied.

---

1. **What does Pooch think about Victor's character?**
   - ○ **A.** She likes him a lot.
   - ○ **B.** She thinks he is a snob.
   - ○ **C.** She thinks he is silly.
   - ○ **D.** She thinks he is a liar.

2. **Which one of the following character traits is definitely NOT part of Victor's personality?**
   - ○ **A.** Snobbery
   - ○ **B.** Intelligence
   - ○ **C.** Bossiness
   - ○ **D.** Modesty

3. **What does Victor's question, "Do I look like someone who steals?" reveal about his character?**
   - ○ **A.** He sees himself as above suspicion.
   - ○ **B.** He is a humble person.
   - ○ **C.** He sees himself as someone who might steal.
   - ○ **D.** He is insecure.

4. **How does Pooch reveal her attitude toward Victor?**
   - ○ **A.** She tells him to "calm down."
   - ○ **B.** She gives him a great deal of respect.
   - ○ **C.** She automatically believes everything he says.
   - ○ **D.** She says she is proud to meet him.

5. **What is Victor's attitude toward Katrina as a character?**
   - ○ **A.** He hates her because she is a bad scientist and a cat.
   - ○ **B.** He admires everything about her.
   - ○ **C.** He respects her intelligence but he doesn't trust her because she is a cat.
   - ○ **D.** He is in love with her.

6. **Using context clues, how would you define the word *scoundrel*?**
   - ○ **A.** A happy individual
   - ○ **B.** An honest individual
   - ○ **C.** A dishonest individual
   - ○ **D.** A breed of dog

Solution
How can Pooch prove that Katrina is lying?

"It's all a matter of altitude," I said.

"You mean attitude," Victor remarked.

"No, altitude," I said. "Let me ask you a scientific question, Dr. Schnauzer: What is the boiling temperature of water?"

"That's easy," Victor said. "Water boils at 212 degrees Fahrenheit."

"Exactly," I said. "And your formula called for the mixture to be heated to 211 degrees— one degree less than the boiling temperature— for exactly one hour. Is that correct?"

"It is," agreed Victor.

"Does the boiling temperature of water ever change?" I asked.

"Well," Victor replied, "it depends on the air pressure. When the air is thin, the boiling temperature of water drops because it takes less heat to free the water particles from the liquid into the surrounding air."

"And is the air thinner on a tall mountain than it is at, say, sea level?" I asked.

"Absolutely," answered Victor. "At 10,000 feet water boils at a much lower temperature than it does down here in the city—Hey, wait a minute! There's no way Katrina could have heated the solution to 211 degrees for one hour. On top of Old Smokey, water boils at a much lower temperature."

"Exactly," I said. "And since you were the only one who could heat the mixture to 211 degrees, you were the only one who could have prepared the secret formula."

"And Katrina lied," Victor added. "Oh, thank you, Ms. Pearson. How can I ever repay you?"

"Oh, I'll think of something," I said.

Pooch's Final Fact

On top of Old Smokey
All covered with snow
And so ends my story,
That's all that I know.

---

7. What key detail helped Pooch crack the case?
- ○ **A.** Water doesn't boil at high altitudes.
- ○ **B.** Water boils at a lower temperature at high altitude.
- ○ **C.** Water boils at a higher temperature at high altitude.
- ○ **D.** Victor lied about the boiling point of water.

8. Which of the following character descriptions best fits Pooch?
- ○ **A.** Smart and determined
- ○ **B.** Easily tricked
- ○ **C.** Funny but not too smart
- ○ **D.** Clever and selfish

9. What does Pooch find out about Victor's character at the end of the story?
- ○ **A.** He may be snobby, but he is honest.
- ○ **B.** He is snobby and dishonest.
- ○ **C.** He is not snobby, but he is dishonest.
- ○ **D.** He is a typical dog.

10. You are Victor's former college professor. Suppose Victor applied for a job at Old Smokey Mountain Labs. On a separate sheet of paper, write a letter of recommendation for Victor. State reasons for and against hiring him.

The Bad Ad

An **Analyzing Plot** Mystery

STARRING
Pooch Pearson
Private Eye

A juicy mystery has a tasty **plot**. To get to the bottom of things, a private eye must pay close attention to details and the twists and turns of the story, all the way from the beginning to the middle to the end.

Do you like commercials? Personally, I can't stand the things. So how do you think I felt when I was stopped on the street outside my office by none other than Dominique LaRoof—the world's most famous commercial director for dogs?

"Hello, dahling," she said. "I'm Dominique LaRoof and I need your help."

She handed me a small piece of what looked to be garbage. It also smelled like garbage. But was it garbage?

"Not at all," Dominique said. "It's a doggy chew."

In fact, Dominique was filming a commercial for Pukeford's Regurgitated Doggy Chews. Their slogan was: "If it looks like garbage and it tastes like garbage . . . then it's GOT to be Pukeford's."

"Hmm," I said. "Clever. So what do you need me for?"

"Surely," she said, "you've heard of Fernando Baxter-Woofman, Hollywood's hottest young dog star."

"Of course," I lied. I'm not really big on Hollywood stars. They all seem pretty much the same to me: spoiled brats.

"So what's the problem?" I asked.

Dominique frowned. "Fernando's the star of our new commercial for Pukeford's," she explained. "And he hates the things. He won't eat them. All he likes to eat is garbage."

"You mean junk food?" I asked.

"No, I mean garbage, real garbage," she said. "That's all he eats."

"Hmm," I said.

I'd heard of situations like this before. Incredibly spoiled movie stars would prowl the alleyways in search of genuine, authentic street garbage. It made them feel more "real."

"Have you thought of burying a few Doggy Chews in the ground and just waiting until they rot?" I asked.

Dominique nodded. But they just didn't have the time. The commercial was set to be filmed the following morning.

"If I can't get Fernando to eat one of these things on camera tomorrow," Dominique said, "I'm up a creek!"

Just then a fancy sports car drove up. Inside was none other than Fernando Baxter-Woofman himself. He was gunning the engine and rocking back and forth.

"Hurry up, LaRoof," he scowled. "I don't have all day here."

This gave me an idea.

"I've got to go," Dominique LaRoof said. "But before I leave, tell me, Ms. Pearson. Do you think you can help me?"

"Help you?" I said. "Does a dog wag its tail?"

"Only when it's happy, Ms. Pearson," replied Dominique.

I had a feeling Dominique LaRoof would be wagging her tail soon.

1. **What is the setting of the story so far?**
   - ○ **A.** Pooch's office
   - ○ **B.** Fernando's car
   - ○ **C.** The street outside of Pooch's office
   - ○ **D.** Dominique LaRoof's office

2. **Who are the main characters in the story?**
   - ○ **A.** Pooch and Fernando
   - ○ **B.** Fernando and Dominique
   - ○ **C.** Pooch, Fernando, and Dominique
   - ○ **D.** Pooch and Lassie

3. **What central problem do the main characters face?**
   - ○ **A.** Dominique needs to get Fernando to eat a doggy chew.
   - ○ **B.** Pooch needs to get Fernando to star in a commercial.
   - ○ **C.** Dominique needs to ask Fernando to appear in a commercial.
   - ○ **D.** Pooch wants Dominique to put her in a commercial.

4. **What does the figure of speech, "I'm up a creek!" mean?**
   - ○ **A.** I'm in big trouble!
   - ○ **B.** I don't like water!
   - ○ **C.** I know what to do.
   - ○ **D.** I'm confused.

Solution
How can Pooch get Fernando to eat a Pukeford's Regurgitated Doggy Chew?

The one thing that ages a doggy chew faster than anything else is being run over by a car. And here was Fernando Baxter-Woofman going back and forth in his sports car.

I tossed the doggy chew under one of Fernando's tires. Then I waited. Back and forth he went, each time smashing the already squashed chew to an even more disgusting degree.

By the time Dominique had entered the car and Fernando was ready to pull away, I said, "Hold on!"

Then I reached under the car and pulled

out the flattened, grease-covered, battered, and pounded doggy chew. It was disgusting. And I handed it to Fernando.

"Snack?" I offered.

He popped it in his mouth. "Delicious!" he cried. Then he turned to Dominique. "You see," he said. "This is what you should be getting me for the commercial. Not those tasteless doggy chews."

I explained that what he'd just wolfed down was one of those very chews.

Fernando smiled—the toothy grin that had made him famous through all of dogdom. "Then let's shoot that commercial!" he howled.

Dominique smiled at me. I smiled back. Another case solved.

THE END

Pooch's Final Fact

Dog food, when judged
strictly by taste
Has no more flavor than
library paste.
But to a hungry dog,
make no mistake,
The stuff tastes as good
as porterhouse steak!

5. What step does Pooch take to solve the problem?
- ○ **A.** Pooch has a long talk with Fernando.
- ○ **B.** Pooch pays Fernando to eat the doggy chew.
- ○ **C.** Pooch takes a bite of the doggy chew herself.
- ○ **D.** Pooch tosses the doggy chew under the car.

6. How is the problem resolved?
- ○ **A.** Fernando quits the commercial, and Dominique realizes that she doesn't need him.
- ○ **B.** Fernando eats the flattened chew and likes it.
- ○ **C.** Fernando flattens the doggy chew himself.
- ○ **D.** Pooch gets a role in the commercial.

7. Which of these traits describe Fernando's character?
- ○ **A.** Cool and calm
- ○ **B.** Happy-go-lucky
- ○ **C.** Spoiled and demanding
- ○ **D.** Smart and curious

8. How does the end of the story show irony?
- ○ **A.** Fernando ends up apologizing to Dominique.
- ○ **B.** Fernando ends up liking the very thing he refused to eat.
- ○ **C.** Fernando ends up refusing to be in the commercial.
- ○ **D.** Fernando realizes Pooch is his cousin.

9. Which of these statements is an opinion?
- ○ **A.** Fernando is a popular movie star.
- ○ **B.** Dominique is a successful director.
- ○ **C.** Fernando is spoiled.
- ○ **D.** Fernando likes the smashed doggy chew.

10. On a separate sheet of paper, write a script for Dominique's commercial. Use your imagination!

The Chewed Furniture Caper

A **Reading for Details** Mystery

STARRING

Pooch
Pearson
Private Eye

The remedy for a tough mystery is often too simple to mention. Sometimes all you need is a good stiff dose of reading comprehension. In other words, **read for details**. Pay close attention to the little things, and the big things start to come together.

I t was midnight and I was sound asleep in my office chair. I must've dozed off when I heard the phone ring.

"Pooch," said a familiar voice, "you've got to help me."

"Winky," I said. "Where are you?"

As if I didn't know. I've known Winky Basset since we were both tiny puppies. And even then, she had a chewing problem.

"Don't tell me," I said. "You're in the lockup again. For chewing."

"I didn't do it, Pooch," she cried. "You've got to believe me."

After I bailed her out, we went to a late-night cafe. The place was jammed with what looked to be other "woodies" — furniture-chewing dogs. Every one of them had that "gnawing" look on its face.

"I'll have a dish of mixed kibble," I told the waitress.

"Rawhide chew bone, please," Winky ordered calmly.

"Rawhide chew bone?" I said. "Since when does Winky Basset order a rawhide chew bone when she could be feasting on a nice kitchen chair leg?"

"Since I went straight, Pooch," Winky said. "Honest. I don't chew anymore. Except for rawhide bones. No chairs. No table legs. No nothing. I don't need to chew furniture anymore."

I'd heard this kind of talk from Winky before. The thing is, this time I almost believed it.

"I've really changed," Winky said. "I'm in CPP—the Chew Prevention Program. They give us rawhide chews that taste like real furniture. It's okay. Honest, Pooch."

"All right," I said. "So what happened? How did you get in this fix?"

"It's simple," Winky said. "Some dog broke into a furniture store in my neighborhood and chewed up an expensive bar stool. Here's a photo of the damage. The cops identified three suspects: one Doberman, one beagle, and one short-legged basset hound—ME. So guess who they arrested?"

I didn't need to guess. They arrested Winky.

"It's because of your record," I replied. "How many times have you been arrested for first-degree chewing and gnawing, Winky?"

"Too many," Winky said.

I looked at the bar-stool photo. "What kind of beagle did you say it was?" I asked.

"Medium," Winky answered. "You know, the stumpy kind. Not too tall, not too short."

Suddenly, Winky started to cry.

"What's wrong?" I asked.

"It's not fair," she said. "My whole life, I try to stop chewing. And then, when I finally do it—this happens. I'm going to do time, aren't I, Pooch, aren't I? How much time am I going to have to serve in the pound?"

"Actually," I said, "no time at all."

"What d'ya mean?" Winky sniffled.

"I can get you off, Winky," I said. "I can prove that you didn't chew that bar stool."

"You can?" Winky exclaimed. "Oh, Pooch, it's like a miracle!"

1. **Where was Winky at the beginning of the story?**
   - ⭕ **A.** In a restaurant
   - ⭕ **B.** In jail
   - ⭕ **C.** In court
   - ⭕ **D.** In a cafe

2. **How did Pooch and Winky know one another?**
   - ⭕ **A.** They were in jail together.
   - ⭕ **B.** They used to work together.
   - ⭕ **C.** They grew up together.
   - ⭕ **D.** They were cousins.

3. **What was Winky's big problem?**
   - ⭕ **A.** She liked to chew furniture.
   - ⭕ **B.** She was a criminal.
   - ⭕ **C.** She liked to steal furniture.
   - ⭕ **D.** She liked to chew bones.

4. **Make an inference. What was the main reason the police arrested Winky?**
   - ⭕ **A.** She was a basset hound.
   - ⭕ **B.** She was a known furniture chewer.
   - ⭕ **C.** They had proof that she had committed the crime.
   - ⭕ **D.** They had no other suspects.

5. **What helped Winky stop chewing furniture?**
   - ⭕ **A.** Medicine
   - ⭕ **B.** Surgery on her teeth
   - ⭕ **C.** Maturity
   - ⭕ **D.** A chewing-prevention program

Solution
How can Pooch get Winky off?

"It's not a miracle at all," I explained. "It's just common sense."

"Common sense!" cried Winky. "If I had any common sense I wouldn't get into jams like this to begin with."

"You can say that again," I laughed. Then I pointed to the picture. "Look at the teeth marks, Wink."

She looked. "I don't see anything," she said, "except marks. Could've been a Doberman. Could've been a beagle. Or it could've been me. Hey, wait a second. Of course! Teeth marks—they're like fingerprints, aren't they? They can match up my teeth and prove that I didn't do it."

I shook my head. "'Fraid not," I said. "Unfortunately, these teeth marks are too smeared for a good I.D.," I explained. "But it's simpler than that. Where do the teeth marks appear on the bar stool, Wink?"

"Huh?" Winky said. "On the legs. Where else?"

"No," I said, "I mean where on the legs? Toward the bottom, the middle, or the top?"

"The top," Winky replied. "Why do you ask?" Then she suddenly smiled. "Oh I see. Look at how high those marks are. A short-legged basset like me couldn't have made those marks! They're too high."

"That's right," I said. "You're not tall enough to chew those marks, Winky."

"So I'm in the clear!" Winky exclaimed. "Hey, let's celebrate!" She signaled for the waitress, then she stopped. "Oh wow," she said. "You know what I almost did there? I was going to order a nice fat sofa leg to celebrate. Then I thought, what's wrong with a rawhide bone?"

"What's wrong, indeed," I replied.

THE END

Pooch's Final Fact

You are what you eat.
You amount to what you do.
For a dog it's slightly different:
It's how you bark and chew.

6. **What key detail helped Pooch solve the case?**
   - ○ **A.** The height of the stool
   - ○ **B.** The height of the teeth marks
   - ○ **C.** The color of the stool
   - ○ **D.** The pattern of the teeth marks

7. **What physical detail about Winky did Pooch take into account in solving the case?**
   - ○ **A.** Her weight
   - ○ **B.** Her fur color
   - ○ **C.** The length of her tail
   - ○ **D.** Her height

8. **Draw a conclusion. Who do you think made the chew marks on the stool?**
   - ○ **A.** Winky, because she is a known chewer
   - ○ **B.** The Doberman, because it is tall
   - ○ **C.** The beagle, because it is stumpy
   - ○ **D.** None of the suspects could have made the chew marks.

9. **Winky uses the expression, "I'm in the clear." What does she mean?**
   - ○ **A.** She can see clearly.
   - ○ **B.** She is swimming.
   - ○ **C.** She is no longer a suspect.
   - ○ **D.** She is no longer tempted to chew furniture.

10. **You are Winky's lawyer. On a separate sheet of paper, write a summary of the case that you will present to the police to get them to drop the charges against Winky. Be sure to explain the key details clearly.**

The Mystery Pizza

A **Sequence of Events** Mystery

STARRING
Pooch
Pearson
Private Eye

A rip-snorting mystery has action, danger, and suspense, but don't let all that excitement get in the way of a solution. Be sure to put first things first! You'll never make sense of any whodunit without understanding the **sequence of events**— in other words, the correct order of things.

One of the most serious crimes a dog can commit is UPO—Unlawful Pizza Ordering. Here's how it goes: Dog is home alone. Dog gets hungry. Dog orders pizza for delivery. Pizza comes. Dog can't pay. Dog gets in big trouble.

The bad thing about a UPO rap is, it's hard to shake. Once you've UPO'd, everyone thinks you'll do it again. And let's face it. Most pizza orderers are repeat offenders. That's why I was suspicious when Barky Wolverton came to my office. Everyone in this town knew Barky. His pizza habit had brought him fame years back—but not the kind of fame you want.

"I'll admit, I got in some trouble with pizza ordering in the past," Barky told me. "It was always sausage with extra cheese. But that was a long time ago, when I was just a pup. Ever since then, I've been clean!"

"Hmm," I said.

"You've got to help me, Ms. Pearson," he pleaded. "I didn't do this."

I told Barky to relax and tell me his story—a story the police obviously didn't buy.

The tale was simple. Barky had been left alone in his house for the weekend. A pepperoni pizza was ordered to Barky's address. Because he had UPO'd in the past, Barky's address was on an alert list that the police and pizza places kept. So a delivery order to Barky's address was all the evidence the police needed.

"I wasn't even home," Barky insisted. "I was out on a walk."

---

1. Which event occurred first?
- **A.** Barky asked Pooch for help.
- **B.** Barky unlawfully ordered pizzas with sausage and extra cheese.
- **C.** Barky grew up.
- **D.** Pooch didn't totally believe Barky.

2. Which event occurred last in the story so far?
- **A.** Barky asked Pooch for help.
- **B.** Barky ordered an unlawful pizza.
- **C.** Barky was accused of ordering a pepperoni pizza.
- **D.** Barky unlawfully ordered a pizza with sausage and extra cheese.

3. What event from the past seems to have convinced the police that Barky is guilty?
- **A.** Barky was an old acquaintance of Pooch's.
- **B.** Barky's brother was convicted of unlawful pizza ordering.
- **C.** Barky was born near a pizza place.
- **D.** Barky was convicted of unlawful pizza ordering.

was suspicious, so I asked Barky some probing questions. "Are there any witnesses who saw you on this walk?" I asked.

Barky shook his head. No witnesses, no alibi.

But the police did have witnesses—two of them. The first was George Roof-Roof, a neighbor of Barky's, who lived in the apartment one floor above his. He called Barky's house that day and reported that the phone rang and rang. There was no one home. And no answering machine.

The second witness was named Wanda Gegg. She also called Barky's house at about the same time and got a busy signal.

I had to admit, it looked bad for old Barky. Very bad. The police theory went like this: When Roof-Roof called, Barky didn't answer because he was pretending not to be home. But then, he had to use the phone to order the pizza. And just after he dialed the pizza place—while he was on the phone illegally ordering—Wanda Gegg called and got a busy signal.

"Did both witnesses call at about the same time?" I asked.

Barky nodded. "Yes, as far as I know," he said. "Do you think you can look into my case, Ms. Pearson?"

And then, it all clicked into place for me. "Look into it?" I cried. "I've already solved it. You're innocent, Barky. You didn't order that pizza. And I can show what really happened!"

4. **According to Barky's version of the story, which event occurred first?**
   - ○ **A.** Police arrested Barky.
   - ○ **B.** The people who own Barky's house went away.
   - ○ **C.** Barky went for a walk.
   - ○ **D.** The pizza place received an order for a pepperoni pizza.

5. **According to Barky's version, which event occurred last?**
   - ○ **A.** Barky returned from his walk.
   - ○ **B.** The pizza place received an order for pepperoni pizza.
   - ○ **C.** The police discovered two witnesses.
   - ○ **D.** Barky illegally ordered a sausage and extra-cheese pizza.

6. **According to the police, what happened? Choose the sequence of events that matches the police version of the story.**
   1. **George Roof-Roof calls Barky's house.**
   2. **Wanda Gegg calls Barky's house.**
   3. **Barky calls the pizza place.**
   4. **The police arrest Barky.**
   - ○ **A.** 1, 2, 3, 4
   - ○ **B.** 1, 4, 2, 3
   - ○ **C.** 3, 1, 2, 4
   - ○ **D.** 1, 3, 2, 4

Solution
How can Pooch show that Barky is innocent?

ithout wasting time, I quickly got to the heart of the matter.

Barky claimed he wasn't home at the time the pizza was ordered. But if he wasn't there, how could someone call his house and get a busy signal?

"I don't know," said Barky. "To get a busy signal, doesn't someone need to be home talking on the phone at the same time?"

"You'd think so," I said. "But suppose the first caller called just a moment before the second caller. What would happen then?"

"I'm not sure," Barky said. "What?"

Here was the scene that I pictured. Roof-Roof called. Then, while the phone was ringing for Roof-Roof, Gegg also called.

"Since Roof-Roof was already calling," I said, "Gegg heard—"

"A busy signal!" Barky barked.

"Exactly," I said. "Even though no one was home. Two callers called at almost the same time. The first caller, Roof-Roof, hears the phone ring. The second caller, Gegg, gets a busy signal. Even though no one's there."

"It explains everything," Barky said. "But can you prove it?"

Epilogue

In fact, phone-company records did prove that the two calls had been made at almost precisely the same time, with Roof-Roof's call coming first.

More importantly, George Roof-Roof later confessed that he had ordered the pizza. His plan was to stand in front of the apartment and then, while the delivery guy was wondering why no one was home, snatch the pizza. Not knowing that Barky's address was on the alert list, he'd given the pizza place Barky's apartment number to deflect blame from himself. A check of the caller I.D. at the pizza place proved that Roof-Roof had really placed the order.

So all's well that ends well. To celebrate, we snacked on some delightful leftover pizza— and let me tell you, it was delicious!

THE END

Pooch's Final Fact

When ordering a pizza
A dog should carefully think through it:
Pepperoni, sausage, extra cheese,
But mostly: Stop! DON'T DO IT!

7. **According to Pooch, what happened? Choose the sequence of events that matches Pooch's version of the story.**
   1. **George Roof-Roof calls Barky's house.**
   2. **Barky goes on a walk.**
   3. **George Roof-Roof calls the pizza place.**
   4. **The police suspect Barky of illegally ordering a pizza.**
   - A. 2, 1, 3, 4
   - B. 1, 2, 3, 4
   - C. 4, 2, 3, 1
   - D. 2, 3, 4, 1

8. **What technology mentioned in this story shows it must have taken place in the very recent past?**
   - A. Pizza delivery
   - B. Caller I.D.
   - C. The busy signal
   - D. Pepperoni

9. **What important observation did Pooch make that helped her crack the case?**
   - A. A phone line is never busy when no one is home.
   - B. A phone line can be busy when no one is home.
   - C. A phone line cannot be busy when someone is home.
   - D. Wanda Gegg had caller I.D.

10. **Roof-Roof is convicted of unlawful pizza ordering. He is about to be sentenced. Imagine that you're Roof-Roof. Write a letter to the judge explaining how you fell into a life of crime, why you'll never UPO again, and why she should go easy on you.**

Answer Key

Case No. 1
Why I Dislike Cats
(p. 6)
1. B
2. D
3. C
4. A
5. C
6. B
7. A
8. D
9. D
10. Answers will vary.

Case No. 2
The "It's My Party and I'll Cry If I Want To" Case (p. 9)
1. C
2. A
3. A
4. A
5. D
6. D
7. B
8. C
9. C
10. Answers will vary.

Case No. 3
The Silver Saucer
(p. 12)
1. C
2. B
3. C
4. C
5. A
6. D
7. C
8. D
9. A
10. Answers will vary.

Case No. 4
The Dry Water Caper (p. 15)
1. A
2. D
3. B
4. A
5. B
6. C
7. A
8. A
9. B
10. Answers will vary.

Case No. 5
The Too-Rich Dentist (p. 18)
1. C
2. D
3. B
4. A
5. B
6. B
7. B
8. B
9. A
10. Answers will vary.

Case No. 6
The Mystery of the Canine Museum Thief (p. 22)
1. C
2. A
3. D
4. D
5. B
6. C
7. A
8. D
9. C
10. Answers will vary.

Case No. 7
The Mystery of the Missing Ham (p. 25)
1. A
2. B
3. B
4. A
5. A
6. D
7. D
8. A
9. D
10. Answers will vary.

Case No. 8
The Petting Machine (p. 28)
1. B
2. A
3. C
4. D
5. C
6. A
7. C
8. B
9. D
10. Answers will vary.

Case No. 9
The Eight-Cent Solution (p. 32)
1. B
2. A
3. A
4. C
5. A
6. B
7. C
8. C
9. D
10. Answers will vary.

Case No. 10
The Case of Love Gone Wrong (p. 35)
1. A
2. D
3. C
4. A
5. C
6. B
7. A
8. B
9. D
10. Answers will vary.

Case No. 11
The Hat Ed Caper (p. 38)
1. B
2. B
3. A
4. C
5. D
6. C
7. D
8. B
9. D
10. Answers will vary.

Case No. 12
The Mystery of Old 81 (p. 41)
1. A
2. B
3. B
4. A
5. B
6. D
7. A
8. D
9. C
10. Answers will vary.

Case No. 13
The Foggy Mile (p. 44)
1. C
2. A
3. B
4. C
5. A
6. B
7. A
8. C
9. D
10. Answers will vary.

Case No. 14
The Mailman's Revenge (p. 47)
1. A
2. C
3. A
4. D
5. D
6. D
7. B
8. C
9. B
10. Answers will vary.

Case No. 15
The Old Smokey Caper (p. 50)
1. B
2. D
3. A
4. A
5. C
6. C
7. B
8. A
9. A
10. Answers will vary.

Case No. 16
The Bad Ad (p. 53)
1. C
2. C
3. A
4. A
5. D
6. B
7. C
8. B
9. C
10. Answers will vary.

Case No. 17
The Chewed Furniture Caper (p. 56)
1. B
2. C
3. A
4. B
5. D
6. B
7. D
8. B
9. C
10. Answers will vary.

Case No. 18
The Mystery Pizza (p. 59)
1. B
2. A
3. D
4. B
5. C
6. D
7. A
8. B
9. B
10. Answers will vary.

Skills Index